PATIENT POWER?

STATE OF HEALTH SERIES

Edited by Chris Ham, Director of Health Services Management Centre, University of Birmingham

PATIENT POWER?

The Politics of Patients'
Associations in Britain
and America

Bruce Wood

Open University Press
Buckingham · Philadelphia

W 65?
PATIENT ADVOCACY
US   GB
PAT ASSOC ?

Open University Press
Celtic Court
22 Ballmoor
Buckingham
MK18 1XW

e-mail: enquiries@openup.co.uk
world wide web: http://www.openup.co.uk

and
325 Chestnut Street
Philadelphia, PA 19106, USA

First Published 2000

A catalogue record of this book is available from the British Library

ISBN   0 335 20367 1 (pb)   0 335 20368 X (hb)

Library of Congress Cataloging-in-Publication Data
Wood, Bruce.
    Patient power? : the politics of patients' associations in Britain and America / Bruce Wood.
      p.   cm. — (State of health series)
    Includes bibliographical references and index.
    ISBN 0-335-20368-X. — ISBN 0-335-20367-1 (pbk.)
    1. Patients' associations—Great Britain.   2. Patients'
associations—United States.   3. Patient advocacy—Great Britain.
4. Patient advocacy—United States.   I. Title.   II. Series.
R727.45.W66 2000
362.1—dc21   99-41546
                                                            CIP

Typeset by Type Study, Scarborough
Printed in Great Britain by The Cromwell Press, Trowbridge

To: Ruby, Bobbie, 'Doc' Elly, 'Toe-rag', and Daley the cat.
'Great family; Great support'; truly my special 'A Team'.

CONTENTS

SERIES EDITOR'S INTRODUCTION

Health services in many developed countries have come under critical scrutiny in recent years. In part this is because of increasing expenditure, much of it funded from public sources, and the pressure this has put on governments seeking to control public spending. Also important has been the perception that resources allocated to health services are not always deployed in an optimal fashion. Thus at a time when the scope for increasing expenditure is extremely limited, there is a need to search for ways of using existing budgets more efficiently. A further concern has been the desire to ensure access to health care of various groups on an equitable basis. In some countries this has been linked to a wish to enhance patient choice and to make service providers more responsive to patients as 'consumers'.

Underlying these specific concerns are a number of more fundamental developments which have a significant bearing on the performance of health services. Three are worth highlighting. First, there are demographic changes, including the ageing population and the decline in the proportion of the population of working age. These changes will both increase the demand for health care and at the same time limit the ability of health services to respond to this demand.

Second, advances in medical science will also give rise to new demands within the health services. These advances cover a range of possibilities, including innovations in surgery, drug therapy, screening and diagnosis. The pace of innovation quickened as the end of the century approached, with significant implications for the funding and provision of services.

Third, public expectations of health services are rising as those who use services demand higher standards of care. In part, this is stimulated by developments within the health service, including the availability of new technology. More fundamentally, it stems from the emergence of a more educated and informed population, in which people are accustomed to being treated as consumers rather than patients.

Against this background, policy makers in a number of countries are reviewing the future of health services. Those countries which have traditionally relied on a market in health care are making greater use of regulation and planning. Equally, those countries which have traditionally relied on regulation and planning are moving towards a more competitive approach. In no country is there complete satisfaction with existing methods of financing and delivery, and everywhere there is a search for new policy instruments.

The aim of this series is to contribute to debate about the future of health services through an analysis of major issues in health policy. These issues have been chosen because they are both of current interest and of enduring importance. The series is intended to be accessible to students and informed lay readers as well as to specialists working in this field. The aim is to go beyond a textbook approach to health policy analysis and to encourage authors to move debate about their issue forward. In this sense, each book presents a summary of current research and thinking, and an exploration of future policy directions.

Professor Chris Ham
Director of Health Services Management Centre
University of Birmingham

PREFACE

This is a research monograph. Its purpose is to evaluate primary material obtained from a unique dataset of voluntary (or 'non-profit') organizations previously virtually ignored by political scientists analysing health policy and politics: patients' associations and support group relating to particular diseases or medical conditions.

A combination of intellectual and practical curiosity lay behind the study's origins. The intellectual spur came from my colleague Mick Moran, as part of our jointly taught course at Manchester University on the comparative politics of health. During it we revisited Alford's descriptor 'repressed interest' as his label for uninsured American patients (Alford 1975: ch. 5). We wondered whether what seemed by casual observation to be a large and growing number of disease-specific patients' associations, each seeking to represent people with the particular condition, were as politically insignificant as that label implies, and, because our course was comparative and we had completed a study of comparative regulation of doctors (Moran and Wood 1993) whether the American experience of patients' associations contrasted or paralleled that of Britain. And we struggled to find any academic literature focusing on the *politics* of patients' associations. In addition, because at that time I chaired a local health authority and had been a member of various NHS bodies since 1974, there was for me an additional practical curiosity. The NHS seemed, in my neck of the woods anyway (Bury, Lancashire), to have had very little meaningful interaction with these associations: was that the reality, or had I missed things passing me by? If there was little interaction, why?

Two crucial decisions about the research framework stemmed immediately from this. First, there were analytical advantages in studying the politics and influence of patients' associations cross-nationally. The striking contrasts between the health care systems of Britain and America provided a key hypothesis that associations would exhibit different organizational forms and behavioural patterns in the two countries, and exert differing amounts of influence over health care policy and service provision. Second, there was a good case for looking not just at the national level but also at the local activities of patients' associations because many key health care policy decisions are made sub-nationally, by NHS organizations in Britain and by a myriad of hospitals, managed care organizations, insurers and state governments in the United States. In addition, individual cases may, through either routine doctor/patient interactions or advocacy activity by an association on behalf of a patient, also influence makers of health policy locally.

From these two decisions emerged the book's key themes: the Anglo-American comparison of patients' associations through focusing on their political economy and political effectiveness. The methodological framework for comparison and for the analysis of political resources is developed in Chapter 2. Because there was no existing usable database, a basic survey of the 'populations' of associations was the starting point. The numbers were surprising, Well over two hundred separate associations related to specific medical conditions, seemingly patient-led and with a range of activities beyond fund-raising (the big fund-raising charities like the UK Imperial Cancer Research Fund were excluded through these criteria), were identified at the national level in each country, and some five hundred in all, most of them founded less than 15 or 20 years ago (the data are in Chapter 3). In Chapter 4 their activities, finances and staffing levels are analysed, indicating that although many in both countries are small-scale bodies, there are several dozen which are professionally led medium-sized organizations, managed by salaried officials and providing a raft of major services and activities in support of their members.

The political economy of patients' associations is reviewed in Chapter 5. The data raise concerns about the cost-effectiveness of some of them.Their own financial accounts provide evidence that a minority of associations spend unexpectedly large amounts on what are styled as overheads – administrative costs and spending on fund-raising activities. This, of course, is not the public image they aspire to maintain as philanthropic 'health charities' working to alleviate often distressing medical conditions through providing reassurance and support, raising funds for research into new treatments, adding to public awareness, and lobbying for more and better health services. In Chapter 6, that lobbying activity is evaluated, with indications of patient influence in some areas of health care (mental illness and AIDS most notably) but of little sustained campaigning in many other areas. Of particular significance here is the lack of effective alliances or coalitions between associations representing related medical conditions: their culture seems to value their individual autonomy above collaboration, more so in America than in Britain, though even in Britain such political coalitions as there are remain shoestring operations, highly dependent for action on their individual members, and in essence politically weak.

In Chapters 7–9 the local activities of national associations are analysed. In two similar-sized provincial conurbations (Manchester and St Louis) there are broadly comparable numbers of patients' associations with local branches, but the organizational styles contrast sharply. While British branches are run mostly by members from their own homes on an all-volunteer basis, the American approach is to employ paid officials and to operate from dedicated office space. In order to fund this more formal activity American branches ('chapters') target the corporate sector far more than do their British counterparts. In both countries the geography of local organizations bears little or no relation to any administrative boundaries used in health care provision, and evidence of effective local political activity is, in both countries, scant. Local political coalitions are weak and in effect non-existent.

To guide the reader through this considerable amount of descriptive material there is, in the final section of Chapter 1, a fairly extensive set of main conclusions to emerge from the survey data. Consequently the concluding chapter (Chapter 10), rather than repeat them, seeks instead to place disease-related patients' associations within a wider setting by reviewing their relationship to states, their place within Britain and America's pluralist democracies. Much of that relationship is theoretical rather than practical, because much of the story of this book has been one of underdeveloped political potential. Evidence abounds of enthusiasm, commitment and important activity in informing public attitudes towards people with long-term chronic conditions in particular, and of associations offering a wide range of significant support services such as self-help groups, helplines and advisory literature, with some involved also in efforts to educate and interact with health professionals. But overall the potential political resources available to patients' associations tend neither to be positively acquired by them nor to be effectively mobilized, and the need to identify a series of 'effectiveness indicators' (EIs) is also identified. Patients and their associations remain largely outside the health policy-making processes, as grateful recipients of care rather than as political partners in the shaping of that care. There are exceptions, but most of the activity studied here suggests that, politically, this is a world of sleeping giants who, if and when wakened, could well become central players in the politics of health early in the new millennium.

My debt to Mick Moran as the stimulus behind this study is already apparent. Both he and Steve Harrison (Nuffield Centre, Leeds) carefully studied and commented extensively on earlier drafts, and always within a few days too, so as to sustain my momentum. I wish that I had had the ability to meet rather more of their critical observations than I did. The University of Manchester was another key support, offering me study leave in 1997–8 and meeting my fieldwork expenses for extensive interviewing in St Louis in 1997. Three marvellous families in St Louis, my now very good friends the Bakers, the Ballards and the Hackels, provided me with superb hospitality to make the fieldwork an enjoyable six weeks as well as highly productive.

Thanks are also due to Cathryn Jones, then a Manchester Metropolitan University public administration student obtaining work experience at the University of Manchester, who very efficiently administered my questionnaire survey to 220 British associations whilst I was undertaking the American fieldwork. My first-class secretary, Catherine Smith was essential in getting the text into final shape for the publisher. My wife's timely purchase of a secondhand computer enabled me to literally 'one-finger' type the whole draft at home, with her continued support.

Perhaps most of all, my thanks are due to the hundreds of patients' association officials who responded to requests for information (my British postal survey of all known associations had a response rate of a staggering 82 per cent), and to the several dozen officials, in both Britain and America who gave up their time to allow me to interview them, in person and by telephone. There was surely an almost unprecedented amount of cooperation: without it, it would not have been possible to develop a 'feel' for the previously largely private world of specialized health charities.

Bruce Wood

PART I

METHODOLOGY AND FINDINGS

1

WHY STUDY PATIENTS' ASSOCIATION POLITICS?

WHY THIS STUDY?

This is the first comparative study of patients' associations which relate to particular diseases or medical conditions that focuses on political power and influence. It analyses original empirical British and American material, including data from national surveys and from a series of interviews conducted in both countries. It is only since the 1970s and 1980s that disease-related patients' associations have existed in large numbers. This recent rapid growth, including evidence of their scale and activities, is charted in this book. Their political influence (both actual and potential) is then separated from the fund-raising, support, self-help and other services and activities for members which often provided the stimulus to their original establishment.

The central concerns of this study are, first, the extent to which these associations can and do influence the provision and the particular content of health care services, and, second, whether that influence (if any) is both in the public interest and compatible with the official charity status that most of them have obtained, usually for financial reasons. The comparative focus additionally provides the opportunity to compare and contrast the effectiveness of different approaches to the organization of patients' associations, particularly at local level where the American and British experiences offer a sharp contrast.

Conventional medicine is central to the lives of citizens in the Western world (who average several visits annually to the doctor; frequently swallow prescribed pharmaceuticals; make infrequent but traumatic visits to hospitals). In many Western countries more is spent on health care than on food. Given the scale and impact of health care on people's lives, there might be expected to be a strong consumer movement. The initial puzzle is why this expectation is at odds with reality. There are indeed hundreds of patient groups (around five hundred are identified and surveyed in this study of Britain and America), but few would use the adjective 'strong' to describe the extent of their influence over the conventional medicine which they consume and medical care which they receive. Why is this?

The usual explanation offered in the health studies literature focuses on dependency. Patients live in the shadow of doctors' professional power and autonomy, with the culture of 'doctor knows best' resting on the apparent scientific basis and complexity of modern medicine. Patients are largely passive consumers, grateful for the time and expertise of the health professionals on whom they depend for treatment and therapy to improve their quality of life.This perception of patient dependency on health care providers who are accorded high social and political status is found not only in the academic literature but also amongst patients' association activists, as will become apparent particularly in the case study of Greater Manchester in Chapter 9.

THE LITERATURE ON PATIENTS' ASSOCIATIONS

This usual explanation of patient dependency is particularly significant, and is explored at some length both here and in Chapter 10. Both intellectually and empirically it is rooted in three sets of studies. The first are the traditional structuralist views of the state in general. In Britain these traditional views see the NHS as a typical large state bureaucracy which, perhaps almost inevitably, has tended to be more self-serving than patient-oriented in the ways in which it has provided health care.

The second are works on pressure groups. General texts on groups rarely mention patients' associations, even in passing. Rob Baggott, chosen here as an example because he is also the author of a major British health studies textbook (Baggott 1998), has more than twenty references to the British Medical Association, several spanning two or more pages of discussion, and five to generic patients' organizations in his broad introductory textbook on pressure groups in Britain (Baggott 1995), but he refers to only one disease-related patients' association (MIND) and then only as an example of a general point, without supporting description or discussion. If patients' associations are indeed pressure groups, they thus remain a largely hidden species. At best they are seen in the key study of the British voluntary sector as 'a "junior partner" in the delivery of formal welfare services' (Kendall and Knapp 1996: 2) though the 1990s saw a new rhetoric by the state of 'partnership' as the state became aware that it could not meet all social needs and was 'rolled back' in the 1980s by successive Thatcher governments in particular. But nobody built on Chris Ham's earlier look at three national groups (Age Concern, MIND and the generic Patients' Association) and his conclusion that fragmentation in the representation of the patients' interests was probably inevitable in Britain. The subsequent explosion in the number of separate associations, charted here in Chapter 3, indicates that he was right (Ham 1977).

The third group of studies of patient dependency is of central significance: the literature on health systems. Collectively, patients were part of Alford's 'repressed' interest, standing apart from the main battleground fought over by the 'dominant' doctors and their managerial 'challengers' (Alford 1975: ch. 5). In Britain, Alford's impressive study of New York hospitals has had a major influence, which still continues. Seventeen of the most widely used British health studies texts most commonly adopted on academic courses were analysed. No fewer than eleven directly cite Alford approvingly, while three others utilize at least some of his jargon. All these consequently choose to offer the student little or no material on patients, their organizations or their influence. Allsop (1995: Ch. X) is exceptional in devoting a whole chapter to the NHS and its users. There, however, she emphasizes the NHS complaints machinery and community health councils; a shorter section focusing on the rise of user influence includes only a page on the growth of disease-related patients' associations, with no discussion of any potential political implications of that growth.

The outstanding American health studies text (Patel and Rushefsky 1995), reviewed in the leading US political science journal as 'a comprehensive analysis of health care politics and policy' (Rhodes 1996), devotes less than three pages to 'consumers', with half of it on public opinion poll findings about attitudes in general to health care and the other half on business and industry lobbies and their political action committees. Throughout the book there is not a single reference to any disease-related group. A major alternative text

(Weissert and Weissert 1996) also views health consumers as weak. By listing as examples of groups in the health care field those representing 'poor people, elderly people, disabled people, and children' (p. 99) the authors conspicuously overlook the existence of disease-related patients' associations.

Though the extent of medical power has sometimes been debated by sociologists and political scientists (Elston (1991), Mechanic (1991), Moran and Wood (1993) and Harrison (1999) are good summaries), alternative theories of power in health care have centred not on patients but on the rise of new stakeholders in the 1980s and 1990s whom Alford would label as 'challengers'. These include government and managed care organizations in America; and government, NHS general managers and quasi-market systems in Britain.

This almost total neglect of the politics of patients, based on conventional assumptions about their unimportance, deserves investigating. Collectively what are sometimes labelled for convenience as 'health charities' are too big to ignore, and, as will be seen in Chapters 3 and 4, they have grown apace both in numbers and in scale in both Britain and America. They employ many thousands of staff, and their combined memberships run into millions. They provide informational and support services, some (in both countries) under contracts with health service payers. Financially they had an estimated US$10 billion turnover in 1990 in America yet the two economists who authored a critical text about their activities (Bennett and Dilorenzo 1994) were unable to locate a single book-length study of them in the previous 15 years. What interest there has been in disease-related groups in Britain has largely been about their self-help activities (for example, Wann 1995; Wilson 1995; Williams 1989; Kelleher 1991; Kelleher 1994) rather than about their political influence, the focus here.

Can several hundred patients' groups really be so unimportant and politically ineffective? Is this first political science comparative study of them destined to be one of 'non-power', certain to conclude that they exert no influence whatsoever on health policy? Are their public claims of being 'non-political' an accurate representation of their role? Such questions lay behind the original decision to explore this new field of health-related collective activity.

Three additional initial considerations informed and motivated this seemingly possibly barren study. First, disease-related patients' associations might have been ignored by political scientist researchers simply because they are not conventional pressure groups of the type usually considered in the political science texts. They consciously eschew politics, partly because that is a necessity for registration as a charity and partly because their self-perception is commonly one of first and foremost providing support, self-help and other services for their members. Thus a title such as that of the (UK) National Asthma *Campaign*, apparently a political tag, is unusual, and in that instance the association's constitution immediately makes it clear that this is an epidemiological campaign, waged against a medical condition, and not a political one, against government and NHS authorities. Far more common are softer and less abrasive titles such as *Association, Society, Foundation* and *Support Group.*

Second, stemming from this, though most of the patients' associations studied here see themselves as, and probably are primarily philanthropic and social organizations, only a cursory examination is required to establish that they can and often do possess significant political resources. A range of political resources, including expertise, legitimacy, access and in some cases money, will be developed in Chapter 2 to provide an analytical framework for the later empirical chapters. True, associations may choose to refrain from mobilizing their political resources for all or most of the time. This, then, is a study of potential politics, of the possible exercise of influence, whether covertly or accidentally, as a byproduct of basic social and educational activities if not as a conscious and distinctive main aim of disease-related patients' associations.

Third, consumer groups in other policy sectors than health are commonly seen as less well organized, and less easy to organize, than are producer groups. They are fragmented socially and geographically: thus, in the case of patients' associations, most illnesses are scattered between sexes and occupations, across areas, and usually with no clear relationship to wealth or social status. And because individuals' interests change over time (in the case of health and health care, people may get better, or get worse and die), they may be temporary or transient bodies rather than permanent, established and mature organizations. Yet Olson's classic analysis (1965), still widely and approvingly cited, that consumer groups are necessarily weak because they cannot offer adequate incentives to persuade potential members to join (unlike interest groups which negotiate wages, prices and the regulatory apparatus within which their members operate) seems dubious: the services which a disease-related patients' association will typically seek to provide (support, advice, maybe some financial aid, and so on) are surely likely to be of central importance and concern to people with a particular minority medical condition?

Disease-related patients' associations have received particularly scant attention from political scientists. And other social science disciplines have tended to be more interested in their self-help and support role (medical sociologists), their service provision activities (social policy, focusing on the voluntary sector as alternatives to and supplementers of state provision), or their financial contribution to medical research (economists). The political science gap may partly reflect their being a largely new phenomenon: data in Chapter 3 indicate that the majority in both Britain and America have been in existence for less than 20 years. It may also partly reflect a reluctance to view charities as 'political' organizations in some domestic public policy arenas: the main exception, a truly pioneering study of non-profit organizations in Britain and America (Ware 1989). This, interestingly, utilizes more material from the fields of arts and culture, religion, and universities than from the health care field when pointing to the variable distributional consequences of societal dependence on them for services and support mechanisms: the impact of voluntary philanthropy may not relate closely to need. A further part of the explanation, peculiar to Britain, is that the existence since 1974 of statutory bodies within the NHS to represent the collective interests of patients – local community health councils – threw political scientists off the scent.

The difficulty of utilizing the pressure group literature for the analysis of disease-related patients' associations may also account for their being overlooked until now. Traditional classifications such as those of Stewart (1958) and of Finer (1966) usually distinguish 'interest' from 'cause' groups (the terminology varies), while Moran (1989) separates preference and functional groups. The problem is that patients' associations clearly span all such categories. They are a hybrid, simultaneously advocating or promoting a cause as well as representing the self-interests of most (sometimes of all) of their members, people directly affected by that cause as patients or carers.

The rise of the 'welfare' lobby in and from the 1960s in both countries highlighted these problems of classification before most patients' associations even existed. In particular, Whiteley and Winyard (1987) developed a fourfold classification in their study of anti-poverty groups, assessing them according to their aims, status, strategies and activities. Their conclusion that political effectiveness tended to relate to the existence of a focused and accepted (by policy makers) central leadership elite suggests that the more devolved and participatory or democratic a patients' association is – and many clearly are – the less influential it will be. This, however, assumes that the target for political activity is central government: in the case of health there can also be significant local targets, including both institutions (hospitals, payer bodies) and individuals (doctors exercising clinical autonomy), which disease-related patients' associations might well wish to influence.

THE CHOICE OF GROUPS AND LOCALITIES

The five hundred or so American and British associations studied are all patient-led groups which relate to specific medical or clinical conditions, defined as conditions which involve regular treatment or monitoring by doctors. Examples of such conditions include motor neurone disease, diabetes, muscular dystrophy and mental illness. Some are neurological, some genetic, some physical, and some psychological: they truly span the world of medicine. Problems of definition which determined the exclusion or inclusion of a particular association, such as the distinctions between a clinical condition and a disability, and between medical and social care, and whether or not an association is 'patient-led', are discussed in Chapter 2. The initial sample chosen for the two national surveys was, in fact, the whole population, with more than two hundred disease-related patients' associations identified and analysed in each of Britain and America, or close to five hundred in all.

After the national-level analysis of activity in Chapters 3–6, the study goes on to examine and compare (in Chapters 7–9) those associations with a local presence in two large conurbations. The areas selected, Greater Manchester (UK) and Metropolitan St Louis (USA), are good comparators because, as will be seen in Chapter 7, they share many demographic and socio-economic characteristics. This analysis is particularly revealing because of the total contrast in local organizational arrangements and leadership between the salaried American approach and the all-volunteer British system.

WHY COMPARE CROSS-NATIONALLY?

Disease-related patients' associations exist across the developed world (indeed they frequently affiliate to international organizations, though that aspect of activity will not be explored in this book). They therefore operate within a variety of health care systems whose key features range from state provision through state regulation to quasi-markets and private-sector markets. In Britain and America the 1990s has been a decade of health care reform with, paradoxically, one country (Britain) moving towards quasi-markets and the other away from them in the direction of greater state regulation to contain costs and enhance access. Patients' associations, it can be hypothesized, have thus had to relate to changing environments and may have had to modify their activities as a result. Part of the data collection has been a testing of that hypothesis. In British terms this has meant assessing how far and in what ways the associations altered direction in response to the introduction of a purchaser/provider split and a contract culture. In America the focus is on how they have responded to the drive to contain costs.

The importance of undertaking a sub-national study, in this case a metropolitan comparison, alongside the national survey material reflects the organizational decentralization (Britain) or fragmentation (America) of health care policy and provision. Operationally, even if, in Britain in particular, certain strategic parameters within which the NHS operates are set at national level, key decisions about the range, depth and quality of health care services are taken and implemented locally. There is, in short, some variety of provision between areas. That variety is far more apparent in America, where most health care expenditure is through private, often employment-related, insurance schemes. Even where there is public insurance, as in the Medicare and Medicaid services, there are enormous variations from state to state (Wood 1995).

Hence in both countries there is scope for political activity by local groups (styled branches in Britain and chapters in America). Indeed, any overall assessment of the political influence of disease-related patients' associations requires a local dimension because influence can be exerted over policy detail as well as at the macro level (getting a specialist clinic established in a city hospital is an example of a micro-level political activity; influencing the national research and development programme to get more spent on research into a particular medical condition is a macro-level goal).

POLITICAL IMPLICATIONS OF THE GROWTH OF ASSOCIATIONS

This book uses a political science framework of power and influence, outlined in Chapter 2. Within this it focuses on the political resources available to patients' associations and on the extent to which they seek to use them or perceive themselves as 'political' bodies. The outcomes in this study have several potential implications for the study and the practice of politics which are further discussed in Chapter 10. These include the following:

1 The development of patients' associations might be seen as representing a new challenge to the established health care interests – doctors, managers, politicians, the health technology industry – in that they seek a voice and influence for the patient. That challenge can be a threat to some of those interests (for example a demand for more services in an era of rationing), or it can be a benefit to others (for example the creation of doctor/patient association or drug company/patient association coalitions pressurizing management or politicians for extra resources). The political behaviour of this new set of actors can thus contribute to two sets of academic literature, that on interest/pressure groups and that on professional power, and will also be of practical significance to policy makers and policy analysts formulating and implementing health care strategies.

2 Their growth raises questions and issues about representation, (both *of* them and *within* them); about their 'value for money', given that health charities have now become big business; and about their political effectiveness.

3 They are classic examples of organizations with a philanthropic image overlaying a political capacity. Surprisingly, few of them take advantage of this situation of tacit public support to overtly pressurize doctors and managers, who have so far usually been able to sideline them by denying them political legitimacy or 'insider' status on the grounds that they are self-interested minorities. Can this situation of political exclusion continue to survive in an age of mature markets embracing consumer power, or will the mass of newer patients' associations, still developing as organizations, start to flex their political muscles more effectively?

4 Common patients' association activities include forming and supporting self-help groups, fund-raising to improve research or

supplement existing services, advising new contacts on the location of medical expertise and quality care, and raising public awareness about medical conditions suffered by a minority of society. All these, plus in some cases open campaigning, may influence the public policy agenda, affect the allocation of values and resources in society, and play a part in determining who get(s) what – three much used traditional definitions of 'politics'.

HOW EFFECTIVE ARE PATIENTS' ASSOCIATIONS?

In the chapters that follow there is a considerable amount of detailed material to absorb, including numerous examples of the service providing, financial and political activities of individual (named) disease-related patients' associations in both Britain and America. That material makes most sense if it is read with an overall awareness of 'the big picture' which it is helping to develop. Hence this final section points to some of the more significant findings to emerge as the book unfolds.

The effectiveness, politically, economically and organizationally, of patients' associations is hugely variable. A few disappear after a fairly brief lifespan, and some are close to moribund, but these are unusual exceptions. Growth is the norm and many now boast multi-million pound or dollar budgets, are sizeable employers and have records of playing a significant part in helping people to cope with disease and in furthering new treatments, usually through sponsoring research. Some employ enough salaried staff to be, in effect, professional organizations; but many are largely or entirely volunteer-run. The majority date only from 1980 onwards and a common pattern is of organizations that were founded by patients or carers, run from private houses initially (with heroic energy and enthusiasm in many cases), then growing and moving from all-volunteer to semi-professional and professional bodies over just a few years.

Some associations restrict themselves to a single activity, typically either running support and self-help groups or focusing on fund-raising, but the majority are multi-purpose. Where there are data on membership (several are deliberately non-member bodies) the figures vary enormously from returns of several hundred thousand members to one association in Britain which claims to have a membership of just five, and to several in both countries with no more than a hundred or two (in the case of the most obscure and rare medical conditions, such as certain genetic syndromes, a hundred people may include just about every known patient). Equally variable is the quality of newsletters, leaflets, helplines, annual reports and other publications, products and services of patients' associations.

The normal public image or perception of patients' associations is one of philanthropy: of caring and self-help at its best. This general perception benefits associations greatly when they seek financial donations and other forms of public support. Inevitably, however, they have a rather different image in the eyes of health care policy makers. There they traditionally have been viewed with some suspicion, as being partial organizations interested only in those detailed aspects of health care which affect 'their' members. This negative image, which in Britain has been changing as governments of both parties in the 1990s have emphasized the importance of 'patients' voices', is important because it may restrict associations' access to wherever it is that general health policy is effectively determined and hence limit the scope for them to exert political influence beyond the level of activities they undertake on behalf of individual patients.

Philanthropic politics is also competitive politics, both externally in the search for sponsors, funds and support, and internally within the confines of a particular medical condition. Competition to 'represent' people with a condition results in, for example, two associations covering Parkinson's disease and four for leukaemia in America, while Britain has two each for kidney patients and for diabetes. Another consequence is a strong culture of autonomy and separateness (or 'turfism') which restricts the extent to which they find themselves able to work together in coalitions or alliances. This is particularly the case in America where the machinery for joint activities is far less developed both nationally and locally than in Britain. Thus in St Louis two quite separate associations worked on behalf of people with motor neurone disease, two represented asthmatics, and three diabetics – and they rarely mounted any form of concerted activity. An executive director of one of the above did not even know the name of their counterpart and had certainly never met them.

Turfism and the instinctive battle to survive has, in both countries, resulted in the continuation of some of the earliest associations, long after the original motive for their establishment disappeared. Thus diseases which are virtually eradicated may still have an association, and the remit of some associations has been broadened over time by incorporating a different set of illnesses. A classic instance is the American Lung Association. Following the successful fight against tuberculosis, this century-old body has actually changed its name three times to reflect medical developments, identifying and representing 'new' illnesses in the process.

Consumers are notoriously weak in the health market (Alford's description of them as the 'repressed interest' was noted earlier) and health policy analysts usually see power as lying in the hands of doctors and managers, with an underlying conflict between the two. If numerical growth is a measure, this seems only to have stimulated and not to have deterred the potential founders of disease-related patients associations. However, in both Britain and America there have been far-reaching market changes since Alford was studying the hospital sector in New York, and these developments have, among other things, encouraged patients, carers and relatives to join together to further mutual support and self-help and to pursue health care improvements. Widely available information, including through the internet, and a growing interest in health matters is common to both countries, and has been stimulated by health systems changes and reforms.

In the British case, where the early 1990s NHS reforms were all-embracing as opposed to American evolution and incrementalism, those reforms included explicit instructions to health authorities to pay more attention to, in official language, 'patients voices' (NHS Management Executive 1992). Rarely, however, are the specific associations relating to particular diseases, studied here, given much legitimacy as representing the voices of patients. British health authorities are more inclined to rely on alternative approaches. They interact (and have to do so by law) with the official proxies for the community (community health councils), conduct public opinion surveys, and utilize focus groups and citizens' juries, often set up by the management consultancies whose NHS activities blossomed in the 1990s. This may be beginning to change, and in Chapter 6 the implications for patient power of a recent project, Patients Influencing Purchasers, involving six health authorities and fifteen patients' associations is examined.

Though plenty of apparent 'successes' are recorded in the annual reports and newsletters of the associations studied, and were cited in interviews with local association officials, the overall political effectiveness of patient groups remains unproven and often unclear. The impact on the health policy agenda of campaigns to raise public awareness, or of research partly funded through charitable donations, is inevitably difficult to gauge, not least across over two hundred associations in each country. One complication is that politicians and providers of health care are unlikely to explain policy change and service developments by admitting to their having had to respond to patient pressure. Another is that attitudes towards illnesses and patient involvement change only slowly whereas this is a snapshot survey.

These caveats aside, there is evidence of some political effectiveness in a small number of specific cases. AIDS groups have maintained pressure on governments in both countries to allocate priority to research, to better care facilities, and to preventive educational campaigns, and they have been studied in some depth. Breast cancer care groups have fought for better screening systems. Concerns of American and British associations for the mentally ill about patients' rights and about the standards of community care services have affected public policy and service provision. Yet even in these cases responsibility for change cannot be allocated with complete certainty: there are too many variables, too many actors in the change process. In the case of screening for breast cancer, for example, gender groups unrelated to specific medical conditions and hence outside the remit of this study, campaigned for mammogram systems as well as the cancer care associations studied here.

Philanthropy needs policing. Sadly, there is evidence of abuse of charitable status (or fraud) in a handful of cases. Beyond that there are instances of doubtful cost-effectiveness and of management failure. One British association was in receivership at the time of the survey. Some others, both in Britain and America, spent large sums, as much as half the donations received, on fund-raising activities and administration. Given the sums of monies involved, and the large numbers of health charities, some fraud and mismanagement is inevitable. In America, the discovery of serious fraud recently resulted in the imprisonment of one ex-chief executive. A few years ago the main American umbrella fund-raising organization, United Way, was rocked by financial scandal. Less dramatically, the St Louis interviews and the British national survey both revealed instances of apparent dismissals of senior staff for inefficiency if not for more serious abuses of donated funds.

Much less unpleasant, and actually far more significant politically, is the potential for what may be termed 'colonization' of patients associations. A common dilemma facing associations seeking to influence service provision is how closely to work with health providers. Some associations avoid close relationships by deliberately excluding all professionals from membership or management, and many in Britain are loosely regulated through voluntarily joining a fund-raisers' trade association, the Association of Medical Research Charities.

Getting the balance right on the cross-fertilization between consumers and providers of ideas and interests is not easy. If it is not careful, an association can easily find itself apparently endorsing expertise in services and products (this includes clinics and specialist centres; specialist doctors it lists on its 'referral panel'; drugs and medical equipment), an action which has the practical effect of restricting competition from alternative potential providers. It can also easily end up by putting the lion's share of the monies it has raised for research into the projects of those whom it recruited to its management and advisory machinery, with no certainty that those are the best projects seeking funding. Such an allegation has been made strongly in a recent study of health charities by two American economists. In one case they found that up to 70 per cent of research awards went to universities which happened to have someone from them on the board (Bennett and Dilorenzo 1994). A classic case of 'colonization' claim the authors, and similar evidence from both countries is uncovered later in this study, in Chapter 5 in particular.

One medium-sized British association, founded in the early 1980s and now with a turnover of around £500,000 per year, for example, had the usual panel of medical advisers and a peer review system for allocating research funds. Five of the fourteen-person panel were themselves running 70 per cent of the funded projects and three were in research units which will have received £1.3 million by the year 2000. Another British association, very recently set up and representing a tiny number of people with a rare medical condition, was pressing for the NHS to designate a handful of hospitals as centres of excellence. This was understandable, but the association notably used as its panel of medical advisers doctors from those preferred hospitals. Large donations from drug companies to certain skin condition associations, and big subsidies from equipment companies to associations working for people needing their products also emerge.

In the American health market, more than in Britain, providers constantly seek new customers. Service on the board of a patients' association connected with a specific disease is attractive to some doctors and hospital managers because of their genuine clinical and intellectual skills and interest, but possibly also because of actual or potential activities such as the provision of specialist clinics, which could generate new revenue streams. Naturally, to forge such links is also attractive to the association as it strives to improve the care of sufferers, and sees incorporating the experts as a valuable goal. Though in principle the 1990s introduction of a 'quasi-market' in Britain created similar incentives, the pattern of colonization is most clear in the cases of research-oriented doctors and of drug companies.

The relationships between headquarters and local branches of associations are variable and the range of differences is constitutionally quite similar in Britain and America. There are varying amounts of autonomy ranging from central approval of activities and expectations of funds raised being spent by the national parent body, to local rights of self-determination.

Much more significant, however, is the sharp contrast between local organizational systems in the two conurbations and across the two countries. Britain favours the all-volunteer branch, led usually by members of an association who have the particular medical condition, and operating from their homes. Very differently, the typical American local chapter is based on the business model, with offices and paid officials accountable to a board of directors which includes people from the business community. Consequences of this contrast arise particularly in the fund-raising activities of associations: in Britain the local community is the prime target for branch activity; in America corporate sponsorship and support from the local business community is far more marked, and the sums raised locally are consequently far greater (as they have to be to finance salaries). Politically the consequences are far less obvious: in neither country is there much evidence of ongoing influence over providers and health policy makers.

CONCLUSIONS

Rapid growth in their numbers has been a common feature of both American and British patients' associations. But this proliferation does not necessarily indicate greater political effectiveness. Inclusion, or acceptance as partners in policy making, has not been the norm, and their image within health care as partial and self-interested remains a serious obstacle. Charitable status restricts their activities too. Their political role (and many associations choose to focus on providing support and self-help, and so deliberately do not seek to exert influence overtly) is thus frequently a covert one. Such influence as they have operates indirectly, through ongoing activities to heighten public awareness of medical conditions, and through patient/doctor interaction and advocacy activities. Only a minority of associations are predominantly 'political' in focusing on campaigning and lobbying as their main priority.

Autonomous action or turfism has been a further factor likely to restrict their influence. The extremely limited extent of alliance or coalition activity is examined later. In both countries, but more so in America than in Britain (where there have been some joint initiatives), literally hundreds of separate voices with an interest in influencing the policy agenda operate autonomously. In St Louis, interviewees expressed little or no interest in working together, even on what might be seen as relatively unemotional activities such as sharing offices or photocopiers. In Britain there is rather more interest in collaboration, especially around genetics and long-term chronic conditions. But something of a cultural change is still needed if the voices of patients, as represented by individual specialist associations or umbrella coalitions, are to be heard in the policy making arena. The latent political resources which disease-related patients' associations possess are indeed essentially latent.

2

APPROACH, METHODS
AND SOURCES

To recognize the rapid growth of a new set of actors in health care systems and politics, namely disease-related patients' associations, is one thing; to turn that recognition into a robust operational framework for their study is quite another, raising significant problems of research method. Those problems were made more challenging by the ambitious initial decisions to undertake a cross-national comparison in Britain and America, to do this at both the national and the local levels, and to focus on associations' political influence. This chapter outlines and discusses the most significant methodological issues, indicating how they were approached and tackled. It develops the overall analytical framework of the study and thus sets the scene for the subsequent presentation of original primary data and discussion of findings.

COMPARATIVE EVIDENCE: PROBLEMS AND OPPORTUNITIES

The first consideration was one of measurement: how far should the study seek to move in the direction of quantitative analysis, given its intended focus of assessing political influence? With 'populations' of well over two hundred patients' associations in each country to survey, there appeared to be scope for the statistical analysis of their activities and influence. For example, their comparative performance in activities common to most associations (such as support, information, fund-raising) could be assessed on a scale of, say, 1 to 5 with the results then analysed to seek correlations, statistically significant differences, and so on. Relationships between variables like organizational size, the severity of the disease, its impact on youngsters, and the political influence of associations could then be examined to test a series of hypotheses.

For two reasons this approach was discarded in favour of a qualitative analysis supported, where appropriate, by descriptive statistics. First, it quickly became clear that the nature of the information available about each association was extremely variable and often far from robust. Even the accounting systems, detailed items of income and expenditure for example, were not fully standardized within either country, let alone strictly comparable cross-nationally. And much of the information on services and performance naturally reflected each association's view of itself, with data that did not always tally between sources. Thus, claimed membership numbers sometimes did not easily tie in with financial information about subscription income; most non-financial activity was inevitably not fully audited; there were occasionally even discrepancies about the year of foundation of some associations.

The precise meaning attached to common objectives like 'support for research' also varied. For many associations this was an activity centring on fund-raising and then giving grants to research projects, but for some it was about exhorting members with rare medical conditions to cooperate by consenting to participate in experimental trials of new treatments or drug regimes. As many of the associations were small, run entirely by volunteers, and were fast-growing bodies, such differences are inevitable. A consequence was that not all 'facts' were robust, but that quantitative analysis might mislead by obscuring this. The call for the development of 'effectiveness indicators' in Chapter 10 reflects these difficulties in obtaining robust quantitative data.

The second reason was that the underlying objective of assessing political influence might become sidelined if the study concentrated on analysing quantitatively those patients' association activities most amenable to some form of reasonably precise measurement, and then added to this by allocating values to other less easily measurable activities by means of judgements about their extent and their effectiveness. The danger was that though the *outcomes* of association's activities ought ideally to be at the centre of a study of their political influence, a quantitative approach might easily focus more on their *inputs* and *outputs* (income from fund-raising; numbers of leaflets enhancing public awareness distributed, and so on).

In essence, this is a qualitative study based on primary (and a small number of secondary) written sources about and from patients' associations, and on interviews with a number of association leaders in the two metropolitan areas of Greater Manchester (Britain) and St Louis (America). Although no qualitative study is entirely value-free, this study did not start from any prior wish to 'prove' anything: early working papers, for example, suggested that it might well be found that disease-related patients' associations exerted no significant amount of political influence and were thus politically unimportant (later found often to be a correct assessment). Nor did it have any expectations about differences between British and American associations. The stimulus for cross-national comparison came from sheer curiosity. America is both far larger and far more fragmented in its health care system than is Britain. Would these two background variables affect the organization, behaviour and political influence of patients' associations?

Consequently, although a certain amount of basic descriptive statistical material is presented, it is there largely to provide background information and it has not been subjected to rigorous quantitative analysis. Its importance stems from the dearth of previous studies of disease-related patients' associations in both countries. This is the first serious attempt to collect and marshal any kind of a comprehensive database of their numbers, size, growth and activities.

Because the key objective was to test the extent to which this largely new set of political actors had the potential to exert political influence within and over the health care system, this study does not seek to assess their effectiveness as support and self-help groups – Wann (1995) and Wilson (1995) do this very adequately for Britain through action-based research in the tradition of social policy analysis. Instead it is based on a framework of 'political resources' which associations might or might not possess or utilize.

DEFINITIONS: WHICH ASSOCIATIONS TO INCLUDE?

The decision to focus on organizations which represent specific illnesses, diseases or medical conditions was inevitably much easier to take in principle than it was to put into practice. As is typical in social science research, boundary problems immediately arise. Two in particular had to be resolved. Definitions of both 'disease-related' (to use the chosen shorthand title) and 'patients' associations' were required, and were significant in determining the number and range of bodies to be surveyed.

'Disease-related' was defined to include all clinical or medical conditions involving regular treatment or monitoring by doctors or other health professionals. The focus was the *personal health care* of individuals. It was not difficult to exclude those organizations whose aims and objectives related to other policy arenas which might impact on health, such as education, social security and welfare services. Many were excluded early, on the basis of their declared aims in encyclopedias and reference works: dyslexia and disability groups, for example, publicly declared an educational and a welfare focus. Others were excluded later, on receipt of their response to the questionnaire survey or after interview: in Britain the Disability Alliance Education and Research Foundation was an example of exclusion because its literature did not refer to health services or health care. Clearly there are many associations representing conditions which span the medical/social welfare boundary: in each case the key to inclusion in this study was whether or not they made some direct reference to *personal health care* in their objectives, usually through mention of doctors, hospitals or clinics. Inclusion followed, even if their main focus of activity appeared to be on social and welfare services. Preventive groups (gambling, smoking, drinking) were more difficult to classify but it was decided to exclude them either because their remit was collective *public* health or because clinician involvement was not clearly indicated in their literature. This debatable decision partly reflects the somewhat unclear definition of just what human conditions are recognized in clinical psychiatry as mental illness.

The boundary thus inevitably remained fuzzy at the edges. For example, based on organizations' own declared objectives, autism groups were excluded from the study, but dysphasia was included. Fertility groups remained in the survey, but the pro- and anti-abortion groups did not. Stammering stayed in; attention deficit disorder was excluded. In Britain the Eating Disorders Association was included, but Overeaters Anonymous was not.

The overlap between health and social care was perhaps most apparent in the case of conditions frequently classified as 'disability' or 'impairment'. Whether or not to include associations representing people with deafness, blindness or physical or mental handicap became a key question. In the same way as above, a pragmatic decision was taken: if the associations' own aims, objectives and targets for patient/provider interaction included any medical or other clinical references, then it was included in the study. Even where references in the literature to health were less prominent than to education, welfare or social security, inclusion followed. The outcome was again a fuzzy boundary with some well-known 'disability' groups (such as PHAB and RADAR in Britain) excluded under these criteria.

The second definition related to whether or not an organization was indeed a *patients'* association. A major difficulty sometimes arose in distinguishing this from a professional body. Encyclopedias could not be relied upon for accuracy, possibly because they themselves were misled by errors made by respondent organizations. Thus two British bodies which initially seemed to be patient groups were excluded following the postal survey: both the Marce Society and the British Geriatrics Society were clearly professional organizations. Much more tricky were cases where an association claimed or appeared to be patient-oriented but was in practice profession-led, or where the senior echelons of an association were a mixture of volunteers and health professionals. Again, in an attempt to achieve consistency across the study, the thrust of the association's own declared aims and objectives, supplemented by its constitutional provisions, was the deciding factor. Quite simply, did the association seem to be patient-led and independent? (The important issue of the extent of 'colonization' by health care providers of seemingly patient-led associations, raised briefly in Chapter 1, is analysed in some detail in Chapter 5 in particular.)

Again the final boundary between inclusion and exclusion ended up being somewhat imprecise. When, as happened in a handful of cases in both countries, the application of these pragmatic and self-declared criteria still left the decision as very marginal the outcome was to include. Hence, in the St Louis case study, the Parkinson's Disease Association was included even though the local chapter was run from little more than a cubby-hole in a hospital by a part-time official who was a full-time professional health worker in the specialist outpatient clinic where the cubby-hole was located. The Schizophrenia Association of Great Britain was included even though it was based at a 'research centre' which until recently was part of the University of Bangor. The Acne Support Group remained within the study despite it emerging that the founder and chairman was a consultant dermatologist at a major London hospital; and the National Ankylosing Spondylitis Society was also included despite its history of being closely associated with a specialist rheumatic hospital (Williams 1989) and it still having a medical chairman from that hospital.

This is a fast-moving and an ever-changing field of analysis, as the rapid rate of increase in the number of associations reveals in Chapter 3. The snapshot of activity presented in this study relates to the situation in 1997–8 when fieldwork was undertaken, though parts of the basic data such as financial accounts relate to a year or two before then. During the fieldwork it was clear that some newly formed patients' associations, yet to be listed in reference works, had been missed. Though a few late inclusions were attempted early in 1998, not all succeeded. For example, in Britain there were references in television documentaries, within weeks of each other, to the establishment of an E-Coli Support Group following serious food poisoning incidents, including deaths, in Scotland and in Lancashire; of a Kawasaki Support Group; and a Hepatitis Support Group. In St Louis the offices of the Prader– Willi Syndrome Association, listed as its national headquarters, were closed, with telephone callers receiving a recorded message to contact a Los Angeles number, almost two thousand miles away. When called, the number appeared to be that of a health maintenance organization, a provider of health care in California and not a patients' association at all. These experiences illustrate the difficulties facing researchers seeking to undertake an accu- rate and a comprehensive study of specialist consumer-oriented organizations, and reinforce the case for operating a clear cut-off date.

KEY SOURCES: NATIONAL AND LOCAL

Not surprisingly, neither country has any kind of official listing or record of what are, after all, unofficial bodies. Initially, lists of potential associations for inclusion were obtained from the *Encyclopedia of Associations* (America) and the *Directory of Associations* (Britain). There being no separate section for con- sumer bodies, this meant working through all 2453 entries in the 'health and medical' section of the *Encyclopedia*, plus a further 28 pages in the supplement of late additions. Information included aims and objectives, the extent of state and local chapters, an out- line of activities, and spending and staffing levels. The *Directory* was entirely alphabetical, necessitating a brief (but fascinating) review of all the 2250-plus entries. The information was significantly less comprehensive, particularly on association finances. From this first trawl there emerged about 280 American and 155 British organizations which appeared to meet the criteria for inclusion as disease-related patients' associations.

At this point the method of further data collection diverged. For Britain it was clear that a good deal more basic information about the 155 was needed, even to compare with that for America taken from the *Encyclopedia*. It was also obvious that the *Directory* was far from comprehensive as quite well known bodies like the National Meningitis Trust and Dyspraxia Foundation had not appeared in it. Further trawls of a pamphlet of self-help groups published by one of the general practitioner trade papers, *Pulse*, of the National Council for Voluntary Organisations' *Directory*, of College of Health lists and of other reference sources including, in particular, the 60-plus membership list of the Long-term Medical Conditions Alliance (a significant coalition of associations, discussed in Chapter 6), resulted in a 'final' British list of more than 220 associations. Each was sent a postal questionnaire in October 1997, with a reminder where necessary in January 1998.

To encourage a high response rate only six questions about organizational structure, finances and activities were asked. Associations were invited to minimize the time needed to reply by simply sending their annual reports, newsletters and other basic documents within which most of the answers could be found. The success of this approach was staggering, with a final response rate in excess of 80 per cent. The 'cost' was four very large boxes of literature which took several weeks to read and analyse, but which gave a very vivid picture of the health of these health groups, invaluable in the subsequent analysis of their political role and influence. In contrast, the HIV/AIDS survey of organizations, discussed below, showed just half the response rate (41 per cent), doubtless partly because there were several pages of questions (Weeks and Aggleton 1994).

The one penalty, apart from the considerable time spent on assessing and processing the raw data, was that there were inevitably some misunderstandings resulting in gaps in the materials sent. For example, the National Asthma Campaign's belief was that, despite the author's c.v. being attached, the information was for an A level or NVQ student's project (in this case family membership provided a separate supply of information anyway). Many of the very tiniest associations did not send accounts, indicating that spending was virtually nil. It was normally easy to estimate financial turnover in such cases. Some had no annual report: if they were not registered as charities this was not a legally required document. One, the Tourette Syndrome Association, sent an apparently standard invoice for £5 for its information pack, which seemed a curious way to attract members. In contrast, 8 others returned the stamped reply and met the postage themselves, while a further 25 used their own funds to top up the postage in order to send a large quantity of documents. All this gave a subjective but a very valuable indication of organizational efficiency and effectiveness within the sector, supplementing the initial findings of huge variability.

The survey also helped to highlight a strikingly positive attribute enjoyed by many patients' associations: the quite extraordinary and often near-heroic energy and enthusiasm which is the hallmark of the new, small, often rapidly growing but as yet still all-volunteer organization. Many, like the Psoriatic Arthropathy Alliance or the Progressive Supranuclear Palsy Association, were still run by the original founders who, typically, are themselves people with, or parents of a family with the particular medical condition.

One of the six questions related to local activity within Greater Manchester. This was to cross-check the generally comprehensive information collated and published by the ten borough library services and Councils for Voluntary Service. A major contrast with St Louis, where fieldwork had preceded analysis of the British survey, quickly emerged. In St Louis some forty or more associations had chapters which were based in suites of offices, run by full-time salaried executive directors. In Greater Manchester the vast majority of local branches were home-based, with volunteer officers. The exceptions were a handful of the largest national associations which sometimes had a regional office, though this might cover more than the north west alone and be based outside Manchester. Branches in Manchester represented a range of medical conditions, with parent national bodies which were variably efficient, active and 'political'. The comparative analysis of activity in the two conurbations is in Chapters 7–9.

Data collection was undertaken very differently in America, for two reasons. First, the published material on national associations was, as indicated above, rather more comprehensive than that available from works of reference in Britain. It could also be supplemented where necessary by recourse to the World Wide Web pages which were a general feature of patients' association activity by autumn 1997 (an advance being followed by many British associations). Second, a two-month fieldwork visit, based in St Louis for the local study, was expected to make data collection difficult. However, it quickly became apparent that adequate national information was to hand locally and could be supplemented from the Web or through contact with chapter offices. A planned visit to Washington DC was then abandoned in favour of maximizing interviews locally.

Initially, drawing up a reasonably comprehensive list of local chapters in St Louis proved to be unexpectedly problematic. The contrast with Greater Manchester was stark: quite simply, no lists existed beyond that of United Way (a national umbrella body, with offices and committees in each region running an annual payroll giving campaign each autumn and distributing the proceeds to a wide range of local health and welfare charities). United Way of St Louis only recognized or gave grants to 36 patients' associations and there were clearly going to be more local chapters than that. Contact was made with city and county health departments (public health bodies, but with some interest in personal health services), with public libraries, chambers of commerce, and some hospitals. The Yellow Pages were studied. Eventually the St Louis list grew to cover 53 active associations, though interviews suggest that at least one and probably a handful more were missed. A list that took a day to assemble in Greater Manchester took a week in America.

Why was that? Explanations include the highly fragmented local government structure (around one hundred separate cities as opposed to Greater Manchester's ten boroughs); the highly pluralist health care system which lacks any one institution like Britain's central government or NHS as a focus for patient association activity; and the absence of the British tradition of umbrella voluntary organizations like the National Council for Voluntary Organizations (NCVO) and its local network of Councils of Voluntary Service (CVSs). In short, America remains organizationally fragmented. In Chapter 8 some consequences of this, particularly of the absence of local alliances or coalitions of patients' associations, are considered.

Contact was eventually made with almost all the 53 chapters uncovered, and interviews took place with officials of more than 20. There were no refusals – indeed the reverse was the case and, as in Britain, the general level of interest in the study was high. Some of the (small number of) home-based all-volunteer chapter officers understandably preferred to post supplementary written information such as local newsletters, or to meet in a public place, or take a lengthy telephone call, amounting to a 'virtual interview', rather than host a stranger.

THE FRAMEWORK OF INFLUENCE: POLITICAL RESOURCES

One certainty is that it is of little value to ask charities and voluntary bodies (which is how most associations see themselves) whether they are 'political' organizations. Their self-perception, reinforced by legal constraints if they seek the tax-break advantages of formal registration as a 'charity', prevents any possibility of an outright affirmative response. In addition, politics remains a tainted, even dirty word in the voluntary sector if not throughout society. Among other things, it is frequently confused with partisanship, or overt support for a particular political party, whereas the central interest of a political scientist is in the exercise of power and influence in society, regardless of just who or which party forms the government.

There are, however, some disease-related patients' associations which do claim to have political objectives. Several HIV/AIDS groups, for example, make no secret of their targeting of governments (health agencies as much as, or more than, individual politicians) for more resources, better health education and treatment and care arrangements, and a clearer acknowledgement of the rights of those they seek to represent. Most such groups also provide a range of services: support, information, education, counselling, advocacy and empowerment.

In America, AIDS activism got more monies earmarked for related medical research and forced changes in the criteria for licensing new drugs (Rettig 1994: 19–20). However, even in the high profile case of HIV/AIDS, where the early groups in both countries were either campaigning or advocacy organizations, there is clearly a perception that a negative image can result from attachment of the label 'political'. Interestingly, all but a handful of the most openly campaigning of British HIV/AIDS groups preferred to focus on their services when questioned by researchers. A large-scale 1992–4 ESRC study identified some 546 groups throughout Britain and 224 of them responded to a survey about their 'aims and objectives': only 3 per cent of those replying 'indicated that their aim was to influence policy changes' (Weeks and Aggleton 1994: 11). Despite this reluctance to admit openly to seeking to influence public policy, Berridge (1996) concluded firmly after analysing the 1981–94 period that 'the adoption of AIDS as a medical problem for society as a whole helped early gay advocates translate their concerns into a mainstream policy agenda led by the medical profession'.

Politics centres on power and influence. It is 'the process by which a society converts its values into policy' (Peterson 1993: 401) or 'the authoritative allocation of values' within society (Easton: 1953). In the case of health care, those values (or resources) are determined largely by central government in Britain, with its dominant National Health Service and tiny private sector, but by a public/private sector mixture of governments (state and federal), payers (insurers, for example), and providers (doctors, hospitals, etc.) in America. The major question for this study is the extent to which those actors formally responsible for policy decisions on resource allocation are in any way influenced by the activities, or even by the passive existence and potential activities, of disease-related patients' associations. If they are, a host of secondary questions follows, including: What activities influence decisions? Are there British/American differences of behaviour due to the structural contrast between health care systems? To what extent does government influence and shape the activities of the associations?

The approach taken here is to focus on the acquisition and deployment of political resources. The assumption is that in order to exert any meaningful level of influence on public policy, associations require political resources. A dozen or more are identified from Polsby (1963) and Allison (1975) and placed in three groups. The first are sufficiently tangible to be relatively easy to identify, locate and assess: votes, money, expertise, public contacts with policy makers, involvement in the delivery of health care services, for example. Others are behavioural: style of leadership, lobbying strategies and tactics, more covert contacts. And a third group of political resources relate to images and beliefs: to policy makers' perceptions of the world of patients' voices. Are associations seen as 'representative' or 'helpful' or 'reasonable'?

The acquisition of some political resources by patients' associations is in part a natural process. Associations normally want to grow in size, to raise more funds, to list public figures as patrons or vice-presidents. They want to develop a favourable image, usually one of philanthropy and caring. They want to develop their skills and expertise. In all these cases there need be no conscious political motive driving them, yet this natural, subconscious process of acquiring political resources has the effect of turning them into embryonic political organizations. Furthermore, their own stated objectives often have political connotations: to relieve or alleviate suffering; to improve care; to work to find a cure; to empower people with an impairment. Such phrases, frequently in the formal constitutions of patients' associations, contain a vision of change and improvement to the conditions surrounding individuals. Though often interpreted within an association and publicly as non-political, these objectives are in reality highly political in that their achievement is often dependent on changes of policy by governments or private sector health care institutions. The desire to influence the lot of particular members of society is the natural underlying agenda behind the creation and activity of patients' associations, and that desire is indeed 'political'.

From this stems a particular problem of image which disease-related patients' associations face.They start from conflicting positions. On the one hand they appear to the general public as caring, committed and enthusiastic philanthropic organizations which deserve support and have a legitimate role to play in society, albeit to a varying extent because cultural attitudes to specific diseases differ (in Britain blindness has evoked far more sympathy than deafness, for example). But to health care policy makers they appear to be partial organizations, interested only in a narrow range of issues which impact upon people with 'their' particular impairment or illness. As the voices or champions of consumers of health care they lack political legitimacy in the eyes of policy makers. As Harrison and Mort (1998: 65–6) show very clearly in the case of mental health user groups in Britain, with their sectional interests they represent a threat to the health care system because they usually want more to be spent and provided. That, at least, has been the perception within the NHS – and in politics, beliefs and perceptions are very powerful forces.

Associations respond in several ways. The most common are to claim to be 'non-political' or to avoid the word altogether by claiming to be involved only in providing mutual support, information and advice, in raising funds to encourage research and to help alleviate hardship, and in raising awareness and educating the public. Such are the conventional headings in their literature. Some go even further, stating explicitly that they are not a campaigning body.

For the political scientist, interested in measuring or assessing influence, this all represents something of a smoke-screen to be penetrated. Clearly, several of the allegedly non-political activities can actually influence beliefs and values and, through that process, they can affect the allocation of resources and pattern of facilities and services within the health care system. There does not need to be the sort of overt, active campaigning of the type undertaken so successfully in recent decades by the feminist and disability lobbies for this to happen. Indeed, that very success has itself changed attitudes in society such that consumer groups now generally command greater legitimacy, and health care policy makers now operate in an environment where they are expected to respond to patients' voices more positively than was the tradition.

Examples of unacknowledged political activities abound. One is fund-raising to support research. Why undertake it? To improve treatment and care, a laudable reason. Why work to raise public awareness? To impinge upon society's belief system so that the quality and/or quantity of health care provision gets reviewed and revised. Providing support and advice services is equally both laudable and political: it seeks to spread best practice from person to person and hence from place to place. Such activity is simultaneously both valuable social and psychological therapy at the level of the individual, and low-key informal collective political activity.

It is the collective level of influence which is the primary concern of this study. This can range geographically from the success of a local branch or chapter in improving local services, facilities, treatment or care, through to national-, regional- or state-level (in America) issues. Examples of these latter include enhancing access to treatment and care, promoting the uptake by professionals and providers of new approaches to a disease or illness (new drug regimes, new surgical treatments, new technology, even the formal recognition by health care systems of 'new' medical conditions like HIV/AIDS, seasonal affective disorder, repetitive strain injury, or rare syndromes and genetic conditions), and implementing new policies about styles of care (notably in relation to the balance between hospital and community care for the mentally ill and severely mentally or physically handicapped).

To sum up, the qualitative analysis of the politics of disease-related patients' associations centres on signs of two attributes in the materials examined: the extent to which an association is in possession of the three types of political resources (whether or not these were consciously acquired), and the strength of evidence that an association's activities *may* have affected services or attitudes. 'May' has to be a matter of judgement, and the evidence will often be seemingly contradictory if only because those in authority in any health care system are by nature unlikely to assign the credit for change to outside bodies.

CONCLUSIONS

A scientific cross-national comparative analysis of the politics of disease-related patients' associations is operationally difficult to achieve. However much effort is put into clarifying definitions, obtaining robust and strictly comparable data, and maximizing response rates, the basic raw material (the lists of organizations for inclusion) is from the outset less than perfectly accurate. On top of that, the analysis of information entails qualitative judgements, particularly about the extent, deployment and impact of intangible political resources.

Alternative approaches were considered but rejected as equally flawed. A quantitative analysis would be either severely limited because coverage would be restricted to statistical material such as financial data, or subjective in that the data to be manipulated would be based on allocating numbers (apparently precise mathematical quantities) through a series of imprecise judgements about non-numerical evidence. A case study approach of restricting the investigation to an examination of a small sample of associations would lack any context within which to place the findings, given the absence of earlier across-the-board studies. In addition, it would be difficult to ensure that the sample covered a range of associations in a comparative study: it might be that those in one country were untypically active or inactive, making conclusions about the general level of patient-led political influence impossible to determine. On balance, the approach of a broad-brush review, with a national and a local dimension to it, as a pioneering venture into a new empirical area of political analysis was the preferred option.

The challenge that this choice of research design threw up becomes immediately apparent in Chapter 3, where a 'population' of some five hundred disease-related patients' associations in Britain and America is identified, a far higher level of activity than had been anticipated. Well over half proved to be so new as to post-date 1980. After descriptive data about their organizations is presented in Chapter 4, their political economy (Chapter 5) and political effectiveness (Chapter 6) are evaluated cross-nationally. In Chapters 7–9 the focus moves to a comparison of the associations' local activities in two conurbations. Wider implications arising from the study are then considered in Chapter 10.

PART II

THE NATIONAL LEVEL

3

EXPLODING NUMBERS

Here and in Chapter 4, basic background material about the scale and organization of disease-related patients' associations in Britain and America is presented. The aim is to offer a broad picture of their numbers, size, activities and finances. Their organizational strengths and cost-effectiveness are assessed in Chapter 5. Any passing references to their political role, resources and influence precede full discussion in Chapter 6 of their significance in health care systems. Analysis of their local activity in two comparable conurbations follows in Part III.

RAPID GROWTH

The absence of earlier studies, in both Britain and America, of disease-related patients' associations creates a gap in that there is no benchmark quantitative data against which an accurate judgement of the speed of their growth can be measured. However, on the evidence of this study, patients' associations are little different from other organizations in that they rarely die of natural causes and they tend, once fully established, to cling quite tenaciously to life – if necessary by overhauling and altering their focus of activity. Some of the older ones have changed their names several times over.

Inevitably, changing patterns of diseases and illnesses can play a part. The worldwide eradication of smallpox, unique in being the only such example, has ended the need for any support group (not that this study found historical evidence of such associations in either country). But the enormous decreases in the incidence of conditions like tuberculosis and polio has not led to the demise of those groups: the British Polio Fellowship remains active, and in both Britain and America the Lung Associations have radically changed emphasis and priorities, now focusing on newer concerns such as smoking and asthma. The consequences of this metamorphosis in terms of competition and overlapping interests between groups is discussed later.

Associations do disappear, however, especially in their formative years when they may still be run on an all-volunteer basis and enthusiasm inevitably waxes and wanes. Four of the 225 UK postal survey letters were returned as 'not known at this address', and a fifth responded that the tiny Naevus Support Group (birthmarks) was about to close: the volunteer officers had completed twelve years of service and successors had not come forward. Whether the four returned letters did represent the demise of associations is unclear as there could have been an error in the address. If they did then one of Britain's oldest patients' associations, the Arachnoiditis Trust (founded 1870: an arachnoid is a membrane covering the brain and spinal cord), has folded. This seems likely: in the 1994 *Directory of British Associations* it claimed only 90 members.

The possible loss of about five associations is more than offset by the rapid and continuing growth in numbers. In both countries this constitutes a veritable explosion of organizations, as the raw numbers, taken from survey responses and reference works, in Tables 3.1 and 3.2 indicate. Few date back to before 1960, though those that do are later identified as some of the largest. Indeed, so strong has been the rate of growth that this might be said to constitute a spontaneous 'patients' movement', with the majority of associations dating from no earlier than 1980 in both countries. However,

Table 3.1   British patients' associations in 1997, by year of foundation

Date	Number	% (rounded)
Pre-1939	10	5
1940–59	14	7
1960–69	12	6
1970–74	18	9
1975–79	36	18
1980–84	46	23
1985–89	36	18
Since 1990	25	13
Total	**197**	

Table 3.2 American patients' associations in 1997, by year of foundation

Years	Number	% (rounded)	(UK %) (rounded)
Pre-1939	8	3	(5)
1940–59	19	7	(7)
1960–69	13	5	(6)
1970–74	20	8	(9)
1975–79	37	14	(18)
1980–84	57	22	(23)
1985–89	65	26	(18)
Since 1990	37	14	(13)
Total	**256**		

this is not to suggest that disease-related patients' associations represent a classic example of a 'new social movement': they lack several of the criteria usually expected in the literature on such movements (Dalton and Kuechler 1990).

A few associations have also merged over the years, but such activity is rare. British survey responses revealed just a handful of cases. The Eating Disorders Association was a 1989 merger of three separate and tiny charities. In 1990 the Asthma Society (founded 1980) joined with the (1927) Asthma Research Council to form today's National Asthma Campaign. Much earlier, in 1946, three separate organizations united to form the National Association for Mental Health, now styled MIND. Although these instances illustrate that the numbers of associations in earlier years would, if surveyed at the time, probably have been a little higher than is suggested under the pre-1970 figures that follow, then 'little' is the significant word.

How surprising is the newness of most associations, given that 72 per cent date from no further back than 1975 (or 70 per cent if the few mergers are excluded)? The final quarter of the twentieth century certainly experienced three trends which can be used to account for it. First, the rise of a market-oriented consumer society, a culture which was aided and abetted by successive governments' espousal of public choice theory as a basis for public policy making. Second, there was the discovery and increasing public awareness of a raft of 'new' illnesses, syndromes, diseases and neurological disorders, often genetically based. This was the era of recognition of rare chronic illnesses or conditions, each of which could easily result in the establishment of a support group by keen and worried relatives, carers or, in some cases, patients or sufferers anxious both to pass on experiences through mutual support systems (contacts, penfriend-type activity, helplines and the like) and to push for more research projects to discover causes and treatments. To get a flavour of this the reader should scan the Index of Associations and note how many of the diseases represented are rare and unfamiliar. And, third, charities in general grew rapidly in number. In Britain there were 71,000 in 1968 but over 154,000 by 1985 (a slower increase, to 180,000 by 1998, followed); the rate of growth was even faster in America, from 137,000 to 366,000 in that same period (Ware 1989: 158).

The American data on the growth of patients' associations, in Table 3.2 is remarkably, indeed almost unbelievably, similar. Only the slightly lower late 1970s and slightly higher late 1980s figures distinguish it from the British profile. The overall pattern for the 256 American groups providing data is virtually identical with some 75 per cent of post–1975 origin (72 per cent in Britain) and 11 per cent established before 1960 (12 per cent in Britain). The detailed breakdown suggests a slightly higher 1990s rate of establishment, but that is almost certainly due to the *Encyclopedia of Associations* going to press nearly two years later than the British *Directory of Associations*, these being key sources. Among the many exact coincidences of dates are the foundation in both countries of psoriasis associations in 1968, vitiligo societies in 1985, and Lowe's syndrome support groups in 1983. Differences of just a year or two constantly arise, with slightly earlier American formations of most newer genetic and neurological associations, albeit with many exceptions. Although in both countries a small number of respondents indicated that the idea for founding an association had come from awareness of a similar body elsewhere in the world, the evidence of copycatting is at best sparse.

This striking historical similarity exists despite significant differences between what might be expected to be two important variables. First, the health care systems contrast sharply. The American is in essence market-based and hence extremely fragmented ('pluralist' is the American perception), and with no certainty of access. This is very different from Britain's National Health Service based on public sector provision and entitlement to care when in clinical need. Second, there is also a contrasting history of voluntary and consumer activity, which has generally been more organized locally and more state-supported in Britain but, certainly since the 1960s and 1970s campaigns of Ralph Nader, more proactive and assertive in America. Yet the evidence from the two tables suggests that neither of these variables is decisive in accounting for the rate of growth of disease-related patients' associations.

Equally surprising is the slow rate of growth of associations in both countries in the 1960s. This was, after all, the decade in which 'left' or more liberal governments came to power after a 1950s dominated by conservative politicians. It was the era in which poverty was famously 'rediscovered', welfare was high on the public policy agendas in both countries, and enormous political activity by a whole raft of consumer and rights bodies was witnessed – from the American civil rights movement to the establishment and early lobbying impact of British social policy organizations like Shelter and the Child Poverty Action Group.

Yet just twelve British, and only thirteen American patients' associations had their genesis in that whole decade. True, they covered some important health conditions: coeliac disease, leukaemia, muscular dystrophy, cystic fibrosis and spina bifida in Britain; epilepsy, ostomy, and Crohn's and colitis in America; and Parkinson's disease in both countries. But this very list illustrates just how far medical knowledge has subsequently progressed: it was a decade or more later before Alzheimer's disease, meningitis and a range of neurological diseases and genetic disorders were either widely perceived as a significant problem or recognized as a medical condition. The Alzheimer's associations, for example, both now large, important and well established organizations, date only from 1979 in Britain and 1980 in America; the two neurofibromatosis societies from 1981 and 1978 respectively. The history of medicine thus emerges as the key explanatory variable, though the (slightly belated in the case of health) impact of consumerist trends supplements it in explaining the recent explosion of groups.

The pattern, then, is clear. Although there are several large, important, well known patients' associations with fairly long histories, the rapid growth in numbers during the final quarter of the twentieth century is a remarkable feature, with the potential possibility that this new 'patient movement' has created demands and expectations which have impacted upon health care provision. It has also led to an increasingly congested voluntary body and charity sector marketplace as ever-increasing numbers of organizations compete for scarce resources, notably for financial donations and for volunteer labour – competition which has implications for the whole of the philanthropic world and not just the field of health and illness. Note also that there are plenty of signs of potential political resources (votes, expertise, commitment and so on) being mobilized here, though these resources are deployed mostly to support the infrastructure of associations rather than to take them into a campaigning role.

ONE ILLNESS, ONE ASSOCIATION?

Philanthropy and competition may at first sight seem, somehow, to be vaguely incompatible, even undesirable when unfortunate and unpleasant illnesses are involved.True, competition for donations from the public, for corporate sponsorship and for grants from lotteries and charitable foundations is inevitable and must increase as charities increase in number, but outright competition between two or more patients' associations, each seeking to represent the same specific medical condition, seems unlikely and unnecessarily pluralist. Although both countries are pluralist democracies and capitalist economies, might not 'one disease, one society' be the expected norm?

Not so. In practice direct competition is, as in industry and commerce, commonplace in both Britain and America. Sometimes a clear justification for it exists because of different philosophies and approaches to the treatment and care of a particular medical condition.This is the cause of the much publicized dispute between competing associations vying to represent people with hearing impairment about the relative merits of sign language and cochlear implants, for example. It applies, with equally good cause, to mental health groups which take opposing views about the balance between hospital inpatient facilities and community care. Issues around 'natural' childbirth arrangements (and other debates about the relative values of natural and conventional remedies and treatments) are a third area of controversy. In all three (and in other) instances the political analysis introduced in Chapter 2 explains that these competing associations are seeking to have their values accepted in and by society (and health care policy makers) as 'authoritative'. However, in other health areas the differences between the objectives of competing associations are much less clear, if not in effect non-existent.

The British Diabetic Association, for example, claims to have a growing membership of over 170,000 and it operates at grassroots level through no fewer than 445 local branches. Founded in 1934, it spent £4.5 million in fiscal 1996 on research and almost as much on care services, including a wide range of literature and a telephone 'careline'. It campaigns for better NHS facilities, has actively pursued a policy of encouraging the creation of local self-help groups, and has the Queen and Sir Harry Secombe as its Patron and President respectively. Interestingly, one of its two founders was H.G. Wells. Yet despite this impressive record and pedigree, in 1982 the Diabetes Foundation was founded, also based in London. In this case, competitive forces are seemingly acting to eliminate weakness and restore monopoly: during the 1997 survey the Foundation was close to moribund, with an 'interim manager', appointed by the Charity Commission, the statutory licensing and regulatory body for all British charities, running it.

A second British example illustrates the tendency of many of the newer groups to represent increasingly rare or specialized conditions. The Psoriatic Arthropathy Alliance (PAA) was founded in 1993 by Mr and Mrs Chandler of St Albans. It seeks to support the estimated 10–20 per cent of people with psoriasis who unfortunately go on to develop psoriatic arthritis (as only 2–3 per cent of the population have psoriasis in the first place, there are only small numbers who at any point in time have psoriatic arthritis). The Chandlers' motivation was that this was the 'cinderella of rheumatic diseases' which deserved a higher profile. This it has certainly got through their enormous energy, enthusiasm and drive. The PAA has its own newsletter, a journal and an information service which was by 1997 handling three thousand enquiries a year. The Alliance was launched in the House of Commons through a local MP, has obtained small-scale sponsorship from drug companies, and already organizes an awareness week each year (an activity which is a common feature of many British patients' associations).

In principle there is absolutely nothing here to criticize – indeed, the opposite is the case. But what does seem to be somewhat unfortunate is that all this energy and commitment could not be directed through the Psoriasis Association (founded in 1968), based less than forty miles away in Northampton and with sufficient resources to employ four paid officers. There is some cooperation in that the Alliance uses several of the Association's leaflets in its information pack, but basically there is competition – even to the extent that the Association's own awareness week is held at a different time of the year. There is inevitably some duplication of effort in all this activity, and of costs (printing, postage and the like at present, but salaries too, if the new Alliance grows and develops from being home-based all-volunteer to salaried and office-based, a common ambition amongst most fledgling associations).

Similar overlaps of interests and competition for membership and funds is apparent in America. Sometimes geography offers a plausible explanation. Thus the American Lupus Society (lupus is a degeneration of connective tissue) was founded in California in 1973; the Lupus Foundation in Maryland in 1977; and a small-scale Lupus Support Club in South Carolina in 1984. The Foundation has become by far the largest of the three, but all still survive and each employs one or more paid officials. Geography can equally explain the existence of several other parallel bodies of which two exemplars are separate hydrocephalus (enlargement of infant's head due to circulation blockage around the brain and spinal cord) associations in Georgia, California and New York; and separate glaucoma (pressure within the eye which can lead to blindness unless treated) associations in California and New York.

Nevertheless, geography is by itself an inadequate explanation of parallel activity. There are also several examples of what is very obviously outright competition. Both scleroderma (tissue thickening of the shell of the eye) associations are California-based, and the 1989 Scleroderma Support Group, with just 1000 members and two state chapters, remains far smaller than the 1975 United Scleroderma Foundation with its 20,000 members and 67 regional chapters. All three associations which represent people with multiple sclerosis are on the eastern seaboard. The tiny Florida-based Multiple Sclerosis Foundation (1986) may be semi-moribund, but the other two are well established and near-neighbours. The National Multiple Sclerosis Society is one of America's older patients' associations, founded in 1946. Its New York head office claims a massive 470,000 members. It runs 93 local chapters, employs 900 staff and has a US$58 million budget. Just across the river, in New Jersey, is the Multiple Sclerosis Association of America, founded in 1970. Though smaller, with 18,000 members and only five regional chapters, it nevertheless had an impressive US$13 million turnover in fiscal 1995.

There is a multiplicity of reasons for this competition. Care and treatment philosophies and geography offered logical explanations but did not account for many cases. Other factors appear to include personal disagreements leading to defections from an association, a preference for smaller organizations than the very large scale of some mature associations, a reflection of the highly specialized nature of many recent medical labels for newly recognized conditions (especially genetic and neurological ones), and a natural cultural belief (in America more than Britain) that competition is inherently a good thing (seen in health care in reverse through the negative American label 'socialized medicine' attached to the NHS).

That there is sharp and strong competition became very apparent during interviews in St Louis. Full details are developed in Chapter 8; here it is sufficient to report that two executive directors of local chapters indicated that their boards had recently seriously debated changing their affiliation from one of the national associations to another, and that in one case this had actually happened – all the local assets, staff and loyalties of the chapter had been transferred. Such action is either less likely or less noticeable in Britain, where local branches are mainly all-volunteer and consequently less permanently established: rather than a transfer system Britain experiences more of a 'births and deaths' culture whereby branches come and go fairly regularly as volunteer enthusiasm waxes and wanes.

This duplication and competition also explains the apparent higher incidence of disease-related patients' associations in America – 256 in Table 3.2, compared with 197 in Britain in Table 3.1; or 280 on the complete list compared with 225. These larger American numbers do not reflect a noticeable difference in the range or number of illnesses or diseases for which there is at least one specific patient-centred organization. The coverage of the disease spectrum, though not precisely identical, is to all intents and purposes very similar, but competition between associations is rather greater in America.

CHRONIC AND ACUTE DISEASES

The overwhelming majority of American and British associations relate to chronic illnesses and physical and mental handicaps. This is understandably so because, unlike acute episodes of bad health, people with chronic conditions are commonly with them for life. In many instances there are no known cures, and medical treatment and drug regimes are essentially about alleviation, relief and prevention, to improve the quality of life. So successful have some new treatment regimes been that 'life' is now much longer than it was just a generation ago. Children with cystic fibrosis (a genetically inherited defect of the glands), for example, rarely survived beyond their teens at best; today many live into their twenties and thirties, and in so doing they pursue active lives too. As genetic research informs treatment more and more, this trend will undoubtedly continue apace.

The rapid rise chronicled here of disease-related patients' associations represents society's increasing awareness and acceptance of chronic, long-lasting illnesses and conditions, as well as being a consequence of scientific breakthroughs in the diagnosis and treatment of rare medical disorders. It also stems from a perception that health services traditionally have given priority to acute illnesses, and from a view that doctors and health care provider institutions were often unsure how to cope with some conditions: the younger physically disabled, for example, rarely had access to appropriate facilities in NHS hospitals.

Longevity of life brings with it an apparent advantage to the chronic disease associations of continuity. Members and officials of groups in the fields of chronic illnesses (many of whom have the particular condition themselves) retain their personal interest much longer than is the case with acute illness where, hopefully, patients get better and are fully cured. Not surprisingly, therefore, evidence of firmly rooted and continuously active acute illness associations is limited. Despite exhaustive preparatory research for this study, no associations could be identified for conditions such as appendicitis, hernia, influenza, hysterectomy, food poisoning or viral infection. (A possible exception was HUSH – an E-Coli Support Group established in northern England in March 1997 following several deaths and severe illnesses from two major food poisoning outbreaks – but its permanence has yet to be proven. There are also some generic women's health groups which include support for hysterectomy patients in their remit, but no single-issue hysterectomy groups were identified from the reference sources.)

It is important to note that the chronic/acute boundary is blurred. In practice there are people who fully recover from skin conditions, from mental illness, from back pain and spinal injuries, and from cancer and strokes. But many do not, so considerable continuity is present amongst potential members, even if not universally so. While there are some associations which can be categorized as 'mixed', of greater interest here is whether any acute-only associations can survive and become established. Only a handful of cases emerged from the two national surveys.

Eating disorders offer a first example, though some would suggest that it is not always an acute condition. The two American groups date from 1978 and 1979: the American Anorexia/Bulimia Association (AABA), based in New York, and Anorexia Nervosa and Related Eating Disorders (ANRED), in Oregon. Both claim sizeable membership figures of 12,000 and 15,000 respectively, but it is significant that neither has managed to create the wider geographical presence that most established chronic groups have developed, or to employ many paid officials: ANRED is an all-volunteer outfit working from a single office, while AABA has only two employees though it does have four state chapters.

In a perhaps surprising contrast, the British equivalent, the Eating Disorders Association (EDA) is seemingly far more active than either American association. Born through a 1989 merger of three very small separate charities, EDA operates a telephone helpline which responded to 12,000 calls in 1996, publishes separate newsletters for adults and for youths, runs an annual essay competition for medical students, and has close to 50 active local self-help groups. In this case one recipe for survival and growth has been a conscious decision to encourage health professionals to join through the creation of a special membership category. This has given it both legitimacy and continuity and has resulted in its publishing – in conjunction with a panel of expert professional advisors – both a set of 'service specifications' for the treatment of anorexia and bulimia, and a professional journal, *European Eating Disorders Review*. The wisdom of such close ties with health care providers and issue of possible 'colonization' by them is debated later, particularly in Chapter 5. In this case the relationship has undoubtedly maintained the EDA's momentum, probably more so than did the high-profile case of the late Princess Diana as one who was known to have experienced eating disorders.

Two other long-standing British acute-only associations provide clearer examples of the problems of survival, though survive they both have. First, the Association for Improvements in the Maternity Services (AIMS), founded in 1960, claims just 1200 members. AIMS has no paid staff, but it has produced a wide range of attractively designed literature and it does publish a quarterly journal/newsletter of 24 pages in three colours. Financial turnover is tiny, and in recent years there has been limited media coverage. Arguably AIMS is a victim of its very success. It played a part in improving hospital obstetric care and in getting acceptance of fathers' rights to attend births (an instance of changing society's values, no mean political achievement), and this success in achieving much of its initial agenda has led to its decline.

Second, the Perthes Association (Perthes disease is a deformity in the hip joint in children which is righted by immobilization for months or years), founded in 1976 for parents of affected children, is also struggling to survive, with only 175 members. Though all-volunteer, and run on a shoestring budget, it still has plenty of enthusiasm and energy and manages to maintain a telephone helpline for support and advice, a penpals register, a small hardship fund, and a 24-page quarterly newsletter (heavily dependent on members' letters, readable but produced without much desktop or printing technology). Here the recruitment problem for the association is one of geography: very small numbers of cases are treated across the country in generic orthopaedic outpatient units, without special clinics which bring patients together.

As these instances show, acute associations have to fight hard to survive. Membership turnover is high, volunteer officials require exceptional dedication, and resources are generally scarce. In contrast to many of the chronic associations, there are few signs of sponsorship from the drug or medical equipment industries. Nor were any of the British examples getting National Lottery awards or Department of Health grants. In the increasingly crowded marketplace of health and welfare charities, these are some of the least secure bodies – unless, like the Eating Disorders Association, they give up some of their independence by forging coalitions with providers and professionals, from whom they originally wanted that independence when pressing those same actors for improved treatment and care.

BUSINESS AND SOCIAL CHARACTERISTICS

Two features of the modern patients' association which have been mentioned already in passing deserve more detailed consideration: the extent to which they are 'business-like' and their links with social notables. Both are significant because they relate to some of the potential political resources outlined in Chapter 2 and developed further in Chapter 6.

A business-like approach includes behaving both efficiently and effectively. Internally, it involves business planning, human resource management and cost-effective administration. In the case of the larger health charities, this means running a medium-sized business. Several associations in both countries reported that they were undertaking wholesale organizational reviews, and the turnover of chief executives is high. What does emerge, particularly in the case of Britain, is that most of that turnover was within what can be described as the charity 'profession'. In other words, examples of external recruitment from industry or commerce were sufficiently rare at top management level that the 1998 appointment of a senior Glaxo Wellcome (pharmaceutical giant) manager as chief executive of the UK National Asthma Campaign caught the eye. This pattern of internal (to the charity sector) careers was rather less marked in middle management, particularly in the field of finance where more stringent UK Charity Commission regulations about accounting systems came into force in the mid-1990s. Nevertheless, there clearly is something of a charity 'merry-go-round' in senior management and the NHS experience of external recruitment of 'general managers' seems not to have applied to health charities generally. In St Louis much the same was true of chapter executive directors, and in addition a number of the outside recruits came not from the private sector but from teaching or social work backgrounds. However, two of the nineteen executive directors interviewed there had been recently recruited from industry to 'sharpen up things' as both independently put it. In Chapter 5, details of the variable financial performance of patients' associations in both countries is discussed, with the suggestion that there appears to be scope for some further internal sharpening up to enhance both economy and cost-effectiveness. In short, the overheads of some associations look to be high.

Externally, a business-like approach is essential to the creation and maintenance of a positive image, a key political resource. At the most basic level of all, the absence of computer technology and of desktop publishing standards today shows up immediately. The organization that cannot communicate cannot expect to influence the recipients of its message. Some of the tiny all-volunteer associations, often energetically led, are in desperate need of investment in basic equipment if they are to develop and command respect. Sadly, the age of the old-fashioned banda and duplicator machines has not yet quite ended.

Like them or not, logos and mottoes are features of modern business which have been widely copied by health charities. Again this is part of creating a positive and a caring image to the outside world. 'Growth through self-help' and 'fighting fragile bones' accompany the eye-catching logos of the National Phobics Society and National Osteoporosis Society respectively in Britain. The corporate image is maintained further, with the latter's newsletter entitled 'Boning Up', not to be confused with 'Backbone' from the Scoliosis Society (scoliosis is curvature and twisting of the spine).

The British obsession with class and social status is arguably nowhere better illustrated than in the case of patients' associations. Largely honorary and unpaid posts of president, patron, vice-president and the like abound and are created to attach the names and endorsements of well connected people to the charity so as to bolster its image. Royalty, lords, ladies, knights and dames abound (and the late Princess Diana's many 1996 resignations were rapidly filled). In addition to the (extensive) Royal Family no fewer than four other categories of personality can be identified. Some associations seek to recruit several 'names' from a range of categories while others stick to just one or two patrons.

Politicians are a second source of honorary officers. Members of both Houses of Parliament are recruited by many associations. Although government ministers tend to stay away from such posts, Tony Blair became 'Senior Vice-President' of the Action for Dysphasic Adults shortly before the 1997 general election; Cherie Blair became a Patron of Breast Cancer Care in 1997, alongside others including the Duchess of Kent. Veteran deaf politician Lord Ashley is, not surprisingly, involved with several related associations but is not typical in being much more active than is normal for honorary postholders: indeed he has been at the centre of very public and aggressive disputes about the relative value of cochlear implants.

A third and perhaps less expected category are the nation's religious leaders. Sometimes one name appears as in the case of the Archbishop of Canterbury and the British Polio Fellowship. But two survey respondents, the British Epilepsy Association and Multiple Sclerosis Society, have consciously enhanced their public image of respectability by recruiting the leaders of all the main faiths. Fourthly, sporting personalities feature fairly prominently (though note the contrast below with America), but the fifth category, 'celebrities', dominates numerically. Several of the best known celebrities have multiple involvements while others lend support only where their personal or family experience is relevant. Comedian and singer Sir Harry Secombe, for instance, lends his name and support to a wide range of health and welfare charities, 6 of which are amongst the 170 disease-related patients' associations responding to this 1997 survey. He is president of two of those six (the British Diabetic Association and the Primary Immunodeficiency Association) and patron or vice-president of four more (Friedreich's Ataxia Group; National Head Injuries Association; Hyperactive Children's Support Group; and Myalgic Encephalomyelitis (ME) Association). He just outscored television personality Esther

Rantzen with her four posts, and media doctor Miriam Stoppard with her five, but the biggest 'name' to emerge from this survey was former nurse, novelist, agony aunt, and, in the 1990s, a government recruit to membership of a NHS health authority, Claire Rayner. Her seven honorary posts span a wide range of medical conditions: the British Association of Cancer United Patients; British Sjogrens Syndrome Association; SERENE (for crying or demanding babies); Herpes Viruses Association; Association for Spina Bifida and Hydrocephalus; Enuresis Resource and Information Centre; and British Thyroid Foundation. In 1997 she also became heavily involved in the troubles and, in effect, the further relaunch of the generic Patients' Association (not disease-related so not part of this study).

In America the pattern is very different, with no royalty and much less emphasis on using political and religious 'names' to confer some kind of social status and image of respectability, but plenty of use made, both nationally and locally, of celebrities. One of the best known cases is the annual nationwide Telethon instigated by Jerry Lewis to raise awareness of and huge funds for the Muscular Dystrophy Association (copied in Britain by Esther Rantzen through the BBC's Children in Need event which has benefited several of the patients' associations in this study). But the centre of activity for most of the more established American associations is the local chapter, covering a big city, a region or a whole state. National celebrities are less involved here (unless they happen to live in the area), but locally the approach tends to be more functional than in Britain. Well known and well connected local people are signed up, but are expected to be more active than Britain's honorary officers, either through regular service as a member of the chapter's board, in the case of the business community, or on a one-off basis for fund-raising events, in the case of celebrities.

Sportspeople and their clubs are particularly active in fund-raising events. Thus, in St Louis the four major professional clubs (the baseball Cardinals, football Rams, soccer Storm and ice hockey Blues) have about two hundred players and there is on them what amounts to an expectation of 'celebrity duty'. The players are expected to spend some time supporting a large number of events, and the clubs themselves offer facilities too. Thus a baseball season involves as many as 81 home games and at many of them up to a thousand of the 54,000 seats at Busch Stadium are donated to charities, who officially sponsor the game, getting publicity and raising funds in so doing. Supermarkets, businesses (including hospitals) and commercial and industrial companies equally work within a culture that expects corporate sponsorship of philanthropic activity, a culture that is stronger and more established than in British provincial cities.

This Anglo-American contrast in part reflects geography. There are national celebrities and national business organizations in America, but the media are (relative to Britain) local, even parochial (cinema apart). And relatively few national celebrities live in the provincial cities: their lives centre on New York, Los Angeles and the like. Beyond geography the contrasts represent cultural differences. Associations in both countries are seeking to connect to the wider civil society by obtaining status and legitimacy. In British society this involves recruiting the support of social and political notables, and of national celebrities with a 'respectable' or 'caring' image. In America, sportsplayers and business leaders command great respect, while politicians are mistrusted, religion is fragmented, and there is no acknowledged 'upper class' in society.

CONCLUSIONS

This chapter has chronicled the rapid contemporary rise of disease-related patients' associations in Britain and America. A remarkably similar pattern of growing numbers of associations emerged, and competition between groups representing the same medical condition also featured in both countries. There were some differences, most notably at local level where the American salaried, office-based chapters contrast with the mainly all-volunteer British approach, and the American use of local personalities to support and endorse an association is more instrumental and less status-oriented. In the next chapter the study turns its attention to a further range of comparable and contrasting characteristics by focusing on associations' memberships, activities and finances.

4

ACTIVITIES AND FINANCES

Disease-related patients' associations have grown not only in numbers but also in size, whether this be measured by membership figures, levels of activities, staffing numbers or financial significance. This chapter completes the setting of the scene by examining all four of these criteria in turn, thus leading onto a critical evaluation of their performance in terms of both their political economy (in Chapter 5) and their political effectiveness (in Chapter 6).

MEMBERSHIP LEVELS

Three immediate problems face the researcher investigating the scale of public and patient support for any patient group. These relate to 'non-membership', to the accuracy of member data and to organizational decentralization.

First, many of the patients' associations in this survey simply are not organized on the basis of membership: there are no subscriptions, no expectations about money or other activity placed upon supporters, and no procedures for voting or regular participation, as would be found in the case of public companies and their shareholders. Non-membership organizations are equally common in both countries. Of the 281 American associations identified for this study, 86 (or 30.6 per cent) offered no figures for membership, and most of those were self-described as 'non-member'. In Britain, figures were unobtainable either from the postal survey or from responses to reference directories for 74 of the 222 associations (33.3 per cent), though far fewer publicly declared themselves to operate on the basis of non-membership. Those that did ranged in size from the very large (British Heart Foundation with a £50 million turnover) to the very small (Craniofacial Support Group, operating on around £10,000 a year). In comparison with America, however, the British associations preferred to offer estimates of memberships, even when there was no heading in the accounts for subscriptions.

There are several reasons why many associations in both countries, of all sizes, eschew membership arrangements. Practically, subscriptions are costly to administer and, unless pitched at a high rate, they are likely to provide only a fairly modest amount of income. So why deter would-be supporters, especially when many people with chronic long-term medical conditions in particular may well have limited incomes and high living costs to meet? In addition, those newly founded associations representing conditions experienced by tiny minorities of the population have no obvious incentive to publicly admit to representing very small numbers of members. And, finally, a non-member association avoids internal arguments about eligibility for membership. This is a not insignificant consideration because there can be strong debates about the extent to which an association includes any donor or volunteer worker, or limits membership to people with a certain medical condition, their families and carers. Whatever the balance of the argument, charity regulators in both countries do license non-membership organizations.

Second, even where there are memberships there is no certainty of accuracy in the figures claimed by associations. There are no standard rules about overdue subscriptions leading to termination of membership, for example, and – given that claims of high numbers can add to an association's apparent representativeness and thus its legitimacy – any motivation to rescind membership must relate solely to the costs of maintaining non-payers on a mailing list. Actively reducing numbers has the consequence of appearing to indicate decline, and it is understandable that associations are likely to err on the side of retaining the largest possible membership and mailing list to enhance their image of activity and support.

Third, there are decentralized associations where membership is organized only at branch level and not on a national basis: in Britain the National Endometriosis Society (a gynaecological condition of inflammation of the uterus lining) operates through 'over 40' clubs and groups; and the Cleft Lip and Palate Association through the 43 branches which are 'its real strength', for example. This decentralized approach is a common feature of associational life in general: it is found in churches, rotary clubs, soroptomists, and most leisure and sporting organizations. Any dues payable to higher bodies to which they are affiliated may be based on a variety of formulae of which audited membership is but one.

Only the briefest of analyses of the data that is provided by associations is needed to ascertain that claimed membership levels are frequently considerably inflated. There are some obvious indicators. Sometimes the accounts reveal much lower subscription income than seems appropriate, given the claimed membership. Sometimes mailing list figures do not square. In a very few cases the claims were so high that a revised, but still generous, 'guesstimate' was used in the analysis of overall association memberships.

Accepting almost every claim they make, national associations have an extraordinary range of memberships. At the highest end are five American associations claiming over 200,000 members each. The Arthritis Foundation returned a figure of no less than 700,000 members and the National Multiple Sclerosis Society one of 470,000. The other giants were the Amyotrophic Lateral Sclerosis (ALS) Association (in Britain this condition is known as motor neurone disease); American Liver Foundation and American Diabetes Association, each reporting memberships of between 200,000 and 300,000.

Using a 50,000 member cut-off point to reflect the fact that America has more than four times the population of Britain, the survey uncovered four equally large British associations. The biggest, the British Diabetic Association, claims 160,000 members. Arthritis Care (with 62,000 members), the Multiple Sclerosis Society (55,000), and the Royal Society for Mentally Handicapped Children and Adults (MENCAP: 55,000) are the other British giants in terms of membership. These absolute figures need to be placed alongside incidence of a disease, illness or medical condition before any conclusions about the representativeness of an association are drawn. For example, there are an estimated (by the British Diabetic Association) 1.4 million diabetics in Britain, so more than one in ten seem to have joined. This is pretty impressive, though it pales into insignificance against the Multiple Sclerosis Society (MSS). Its 55,000 members support a condition that is thought to be borne by about 80,000 people in Britain (not all members have the condition of course: MSS is typical of most associations in welcoming as members all who 'subscribe to the common goals of the charity').

The very high motor neurone disease (ALS in America) membership figure claimed in America shows some of the problems of comparison. Strictly speaking the UK Motor Neurone Disease Association has only some 6000 paid-up members, but its publicity claims that it also has 40,000 supporters. As this is a brain and spinal cord degenerative condition which is limited at any one time to an estimated 5000 people in Britain, both figures are anyway very impressive. That the American ALS Association can claim 250,000 members is a reflection of the twin American obsessions with baseball and with sporting heroes. Lou Gehrig was one of baseball's 'sporting legends'. Nicknamed 'The Iron Horse', he was 1st base for the New York Yankees between the wars. He was forced into retirement in 1939 by the onset of the disease, living for only two more years. To this day few use the medical name. In America this is 'Lou Gehrig's Disease'.

If the comprehensiveness of membership is important then many of the smaller groups, representing very rare conditions, are probably even more representative than the giants cited above. For example, only 1000 people have been diagnosed in Britain as having progressive supranuclear palsy (PSP, a neuro-degenerative disease), but the PSP Association (founded in 1994 by a couple – sadly, the wife died from it a year later) has 778 members. Very comparably, in terms of populations, the 1990 American Society for PSP has four times the membership (3000). All known British families affected by Lowe's syndrome – fewer than 20 – are members of the Indiana-based LS Association which (uniquely in this survey) is organized internationally rather than country-by-country because of the tiny numbers. Not many smaller groups exist, though the *Directory of British Associations* reported a membership of only 5 in the case of the Munchausen's Syndrome Self-help Group, founded in 1982 but a non-respondent to the 1997 questionnaire. Three other tiny British associations reported fewer than 100 members: the Congenital CMV (cyto megalo virus) Association (a flu-like condition which can lead to physical, behavioural or learning problems in babies); the British Diastasis Symphisis Pubis Support Group (a pelvic ligament condition); and the TAR Syndrome Support Group (a blood platelets condition associated with the absence of the forearm bone); with many more with memberships of below 250.

America, too, has its minnows, with four reports of 100 members or fewer: the Freeman–Sheldon Support Group (a cranio-facial abnormality) based at Salt Lake City and founded in 1982; the New York-based American Skin Association, founded in 1987 and one of no fewer than seven separate dermatology groups; the Association of Neuro-metabolic disorders, founded in Ohio in 1980, in a field (metabolic disorders) where at least twelve other highly specialized associations have been formed subsequently; and the Colorado-based National Support Group for PM/DM founded in 1989. PM/DM is a neurological disorder, another area of medicine experiencing an enormous growth of numbers of associations: America now has 44 separate associations for such disorders.

From small beginnings can grow large and successful associations. Although a handful show clear signs of decline – the National Ankylosing Spondylitis Society (a progressive rheumatic disease, usually spinal) with now under 8000 members from a peak of around 11,500 being one British instance – the overwhelming trend in both Britain and America is one of growing memberships. In certain cases there are very rapid rates of increase. The tiny Sickle Cell Society in Britain, formed by patients and parents with some professionals in support in 1979, was close to moribund with only 75 paid-up members in 1995, but it was able to report 200 a year later. The Myotonic Dystrophy Support Group grew from 220 to 320 in 1996–7. The Fragile X Society (a genetic learning disability syndrome) began with just 50 members in 1989 and now has 957; and Behcet's Syndrome Society (an over-reactive immune system causing inflammation) recorded 580 members in 1995, 700 a year later and 830 in 1997. As statistics suggest that only about 350 have this condition, such growth testifies the active enthusiasm which can be found in all-volunteer organizations (which all these British examples are), and Behcet's Syndrome Society (BSS) looks to be stronger than the Arizona-based American Behcet's Disease Association which was not founded until 1989, six years later than BSS, and which provided no indication of membership or of serious activity.

Many larger associations, too, are growing. A 46 per cent increase in membership (to 9687) in one year was reported by the British Tinnitus Association in 1997, while the British Epilepsy Association grew from 19,362 to 21,000 that same year (1996–7), and the Parkinson's Disease Society of Britain from 22,000 to 25,000. For these established groups, measures of staffing and financial activity (analysed below) are more appropriate, but for the medium-sized association growth has a more fundamental significance. There comes a point where the transition from all-volunteer to part-professional becomes necessary. This transition is frequently a major ambition of the founders in both countries, though more so at the local chapter level in America as even the smallest of America's national organizations usually report having one paid member of staff virtually from the outset, in contrast to the British all-volunteer approach until the workload becomes too great.

The Ménière's Society is a typical British example of this transition. Founded in 1984 by a sufferer of Ménière's disease (this condition is tinnitus, vertigo and deafness in combination, first described in 1861) who discovered that in Holland there was a telephone network giving mutual support, it ran on an all-volunteer basis for ten years until a three-year government grant, reducing annually over that time, was obtained for the employment of a paid officer and an assistant. Already growing steadily, the new officers stimulated a 33 per cent growth to almost 4000 members in the 1996–7 fiscal year, and the Society launched a fund-raising appeal which increased donations by £15,000. In all, its income rose from £42,000 to £90,000 in the year. Such an increase is essential if the Society is to be able to maintain its paid staff when the pump-priming grant (of which there are up to twenty similar British examples, discussed below) ends. Other recent British instances of the transition to a salary-based organization include the Cardiomyopathy Association (an inherited disease of the heart muscle, a common cause of sudden death in the young) and the Interstitial Cystitis Support Group. That the state should actively promote the growth of patients' associations is an issue for discussion in Chapter 10.

The 195 American associations which furnished membership numbers claimed a total of 3.7 million members, over half of whom were in the 'big 5' whose details were reported earlier (page 53). These are, of course, national figures and many of the chapters have additional local members who either do not or, depending on the association's constitution, cannot join nationally (the latter is, of course, always the case with the 86 non-membership bodies). In Britain, data for those reporting membership numbers suggest a total of about 845,000 members, or an almost identical ratio to America per million of the population. In Britain, the 'big 4' (see page 53) account for around 40 per cent of this total. Coupled with the finding in Chapter 3 of fairly similar numbers of associations and coverage of medical conditions, there now emerges a very comparable incidence of memberships in the two countries.

AIMS AND ACTIVITIES

Equally comparable are the official aims and objectives of most British and American patients' associations. To a large extent this reflects the laws about receipt of charity status and the attendant tax breaks. Almost all of the more established associations seek this registration, in America known after the relevant legislative sub-section as 'C–510(3) status', as, among other considerations, it offers both a label of respectability and, more importantly perhaps, a tax rebate on donated funds. For this study, two immediate consequences relate to the common language and expressions of association literature, and to the common self-claim of being 'non-political'.

At first sight, patient association literature about activities has a distinct sameness about it. In Britain phrases such as 'promoting the relief of suffering' remain quite commonplace yet are curiously dated linguistically (modern political correctness has led 'suffering' to be replaced by 'people with . . .'). The older terminology reflects the wording of early legislation on charities. Most of the associations studied also include the provision of 'advice', 'support', 'information' and 'education' at the top of their stated objectives, often followed by the 'promotion of research' through fund-raising. Only lower in the list are phrases such as 'raising public awareness' and, very occasionally, 'campaigning', both of which can be interpreted as political activities, given the earlier definition of 'political' as influencing the allocation of values and resources within society. The potentially ambiguous but also often-used term 'advocacy' almost always relates to helping individual patients seeking social security entitlements. In America there is a similar linguistic pattern, though the exact phraseology is slightly different and 'advocacy' can include collective lobbying. In both countries the regulatory agencies overseeing charities accept this mixture of philanthropic and political activity on the basis that the latter is non-partisan (that is the aims are general and not directed at any single political party but at governments and at public opinions or attitudes towards particular medical conditions).

For this study those activities involving the provision of basic advice and support services are not of central importance because the focus is political influence. Nevertheless it would be unfair to underestimate the significance to both associations and people with conditions of such activities. Enormous efforts go into this work, and activity levels are increasing overall. The standard of literature is professional in the case of the larger groups, while the newer and smaller ones publish leaflets and circulate newsletters notable for their empathy with the circumstances faced by many of the intended readers.

In both countries self-help and support groups, and penpal, 'buddy' and other contact schemes abound in an attempt to help people to come to terms with their condition. Particularly noteworthy are the plethora of telephone helplines, many of them dating only from the 1990s. The British Epilepsy Association, for example, recorded 43,000 helpline queries in 1996. Interestingly its detailed breakdown revealed that some 8500 of these calls for advice came not from patients but from doctors, teachers and social workers involved in the care of epileptics. Its 24-page quarterly newsletter, quite glossy and very accessible in style, has a mailing list of 90,000 though there are only 21,000 paid-up members. The National Eczema Society fielded 23,500 queries in 1996, of which some 70 per cent were by telephone. The Cardiomyopathy Association experienced a 60 per cent increase in enquiries in 1996 alone. Dozens of other British associations reported 5000–10,000 or so telephone calls a year to helplines, including the Continence Foundation and Breast Cancer Care, while even the Toxoplasmosis Trust (a parasitic infection of particular concern during pregnancy) received 5000 calls despite there being only around 1400 diagnosed cases per year.

Telephone helplines, staffed by either qualified health care workers (often on a voluntary and unpaid basis in the case of the smaller associations) or trained volunteers, have escalated both in number and in uptake. They consume a lot of resources, in terms of both manpower and money. The (UK) National Endometriosis Society, for example, had a 52 per cent increase in calls in one year to its daily line which operates only in the evening. Although the service is staffed on a trained but all-volunteer basis, the average call received cost the Society around £1.70 in 1996–7. The Eating Disorders Association was seeking to install more lines as its growth to 12,000 annual calls meant that it was operating at capacity. Given the activity levels in this field of information and support, there appears to have been scope for the British government to have built on the solid bases evident here by working in partnership with patients' associations (a few of whose helplines it has actually funded through pump-priming grants). Instead it opted for duplication through a quite separate, official, all-purpose NHS helpline in its White Paper proposals for NHS reform (Secretary of State for Health 1997: para 1.11).

Helplines and other support systems could, of course, be interpreted as political activities in that they indirectly pressurize health care payers and providers by raising patients' expectations and demands through improving their knowledge of medical conditions and treatments. Such covert politics is very much the consequence rather than the intention of those who work, paid and unpaid, for disease-related associations. Rightly they would point to the signs here of tremendous social innovation, using communications technology to create new social networks. Many, indeed, already utilize web pages to supplement their basic support services, and many others plan to do likewise. Associations themselves generally do not view these activities as political because their aim is the provision of comfort, support and advice to those they represent.

Some do refer to 'campaigning' activity, but much of this targets individual behaviour rather than health care institutions, as in the examples of kidney, liver and heart groups working to encourage organ donors to come forward or cancer charities urging women to undertake breast self-examination. Thus some 29 per cent of the (UK) National Eczema Society's 1996 expenditure was on 'campaigns' but these were mostly to empower individuals through better education and information. Some was more clearly political, targeting governments and institutions, in this case through funding a coalition of patients' associations entitled the Skin Care Campaign.The (UK) National Kidney Federation also worked jointly (with the Renal Association) and devoted considerable resources to campaigning. The main item in its 1996 annual report related to the attempt to exert pressure on the Department of Health to implement the recommendations of a renal review, not least because the numbers of transplants had fallen to the lowest level since the mid-1980s and the waiting list had risen rapidly, from 3700 in 1988 to 5600 in 1996. Alliances of separate associations, more common and purposeful in Britain than in America, are discussed in Chapter 6.

Other British associations working to change government policy included the Coeliac Society, about food labelling laws, and the Child Growth Foundation which claimed that back in 1993 it 'won the battle to guarantee' that growth charts were universally used for babies in the UK. Responses varied in their conviction. The British Snoring and Sleep Apnoea Association claimed that it sought to 'petition government and the NHS for better facilities and greater funding for this area of medicine', though the information produced suggested that actual activity was a good deal more low-key than these words might imply. In contrast, the Stroke Association organized a mass lobby of Parliament in October 1997, delivering a petition containing almost 100,000 names to Downing Street calling for specialized stroke units and home care services under the slogan calling for 'good practice to become national practice'.

In interviews there was ambivalence about the political role of patients' associations. Officers naturally tended to begin by claiming that their organizations not only had to be (under charity rules) but actually were non-political. As always, the distinction between political and partisan had to be made, to focus on power and influence in the health care systems in general. Although what has earlier been termed 'covert politics' or influence through the dissemination of information and sponsorship of research was identified, widespread reluctance to accept the notion of overt politics and political campaigning remained. The common explanation was that this was simply not possible under charity laws, but this was no more than a convenient refuge. Many well known health-related bodies in both America and Britain at the forefront of political campaigning for treatment rights, particularly in the fields of HIV/AIDS and mental health, are registered charities. And, when pressed, most charity officials were well aware of the existence of certain rules of thumb about political activities. In America, for example, they suggested that a charity's accounts could show up to 20–25 per cent of income spent on campaigning activities under the normal Internal Revenue Service interpretation of charity status rules.

STAFFING

Measured in terms of employment, the biggest of the American patients' associations are extremely large organizations, with hundreds of officials on the payroll. Returns include no fewer than 829 staff working for the American Diabetes Association, a massive 1000 for the Muscular Dystrophy Association, 900 for the National Multiple Sclerosis Society, 600 for the Arthritis Foundation, and 375 for the Leukemia Society of America.

Some care is needed in interpreting official returns however, for three main reasons. First, some health charities (not those cited above) are known to include volunteers in their numbers. Thus Fibrodysplasia Ossificans, an association founded in 1988 to support those with a very rare disease (deposit of new bone behind the eye which can cause blindness in babies), reported 13 staff servicing just 105 members. Second, numbers are normally a head count rather than an adjusted total for 'full-time equivalents', and part-time charity work is commonplace in both countries. Third, the American associations operate through different constitutions.

Some of the seemingly largest organizations employ all local chapter staff direct from headquarters whereas others, the majority, operate through a devolved structure whereby each chapter employs its own officials who do not appear on national returns. An additional complication is that national returns may or may not include regional officials responsible for supporting local chapters across several cities and states.

The 164 American associations which reported on staffing directly employed only some 5422 officials. The five largest, listed above, accounted for two-thirds. Much more typical are returns of 1–5 employees at headquarters with no information about chapter staff. The Sickle Cell Disease Association, for example, has 6 staff but its 86 chapters are known each to employ at least 1 person, as in St Louis. The 9 Lupus Foundation of America staff include its 4 regional officers but not those of its 100 or so chapters. Alzheimer's Association reported only 115 staff but the St Louis chapter alone (one of 218) employed some 25 more.

In comparison, most British associations are far smaller employers, even after taking the Anglo-American overall population size into account. For a start, more of the smaller associations remain run on an all-volunteer basis in Britain when compared with America. The larger employers include the Association for Spina Bifida and Hydrocephalus. With a budget placing it in the top twenty in terms of turnover, it has 98 staff of whom a majority (51) are part-timers. Many of those are not based at headquarters because the Association provides some of its flagship services through a team of regional specialist advisers (collectively named START) offering local rehabilitation and training. However, in this survey the giant was SCOPE (for people with cerebral palsy). SCOPE was running sixteen schools, centres and employment programmes. It employed 3942 staff of whom 2286 were classed as direct service providers and a further 1122 worked in its chain of shops, found in most town centres. Only MENCAP, the Royal Society for Mentally Handicapped Children and Adults, had a larger budget and workforce (5000 employees) amongst the health charities included here: it runs three colleges of further education, care homes for 3000 residents and 700 local Gateway Clubs across the country. MENCAP's services are more akin to those provided by the traditional charities for the disabled which preceded state welfare provision, and its focus reflects the progressive demedicalization of mental handicap.

The British survey material shows a clear pattern of staff growth, particularly in the smaller and newer associations. The National

Osteoporosis Society was founded only in 1986, initially with just 2 members of staff: by 1996 it had 25 employees including 4 specialist nurses. The ME Association grew from 1 to 13 staff between 1981 and 1996; the Manic Depression Fellowship from nothing (founded only in 1983) to 12, half of whom themselves have the condition. Founded in 1986, the Hodgkin's Disease and Lymphoma Association appointed its first full-time paid director only in 1994 but by 1997 had 13 on the payroll (of whom 10 were part-timers). Many of the large number of new and all-volunteer associations in Britain have as a key objective the establishment of an office in place of space in the private homes of founders. This ambition they shared with the St Louis all-volunteer chapters, although these were relatively few because most have paid staff and an office base.

A far more interesting contrast between America and Britain lies in the relationship between the state and patients' associations. In Britain there has been (in the 1990s but the origins lay a decade or more earlier) a clear government policy of providing public funds to encourage these fledgling associations to mature from being home-based and all-volunteer organizations towards salaried professional, office-based management. This entirely bi-partisan policy has been implemented through both grants made from Department of Health funds and, recently, awards from the National Lottery Charities Board. In the next section more details will emerge. America has no equivalent public policy of infrastructure support for patients' associations.

FINANCES

Analysis of the spending of the associations studied here inevitably reveals enormous variation.The smallest have budgets of below one thousand pounds or dollars per year and are both all-volunteer and barely surviving. They include the Freeman–Sheldon Support Group and the Fatty Oxidation Disorders (FOD) Family Support Group in America. The former is a cranio-facial abnormality, and the Salt Lake City-based association, founded in 1982, boasts just 91 members and 1 staff. There are 120 members of FOD (a metabolic disorder); its one-person office is in North Carolina, where it was founded in 1991. Of comparable size in Britain are the Telangiectasia Self Help Group (a genetic fault causing nose and internal bleeding), run from a High Wycombe house almost on a one-woman basis and with 200 members; and the Cushing Care Helpline, established in 1991 literally as a labour of love by the Preston mother of a child with this hormonal complaint requiring radiotherapy or surgery – she has answered around 1000 enquiries in six years and has self-funded the service with the help of a few small donations, mainly from a specialist cancer hospital in Manchester.

Unfortunately only 112 of the 281 American associations provided detailed information about their budgets, compared with 161 in Britain. Total expenditures of respondent associations in both countries are analysed in Table 4.1. The amounts are expressed in pounds sterling. An exchange rate of 1.5 dollars to the pound, very close to the actual exchange rate in 1996, the year of most of the data, has been used. This rough-and-ready conversion does not reflect purchasing power precisely but the categories of spending used in Table 4.1 are wide enough to give an acceptably accurate picture of comparative spending levels.

The data in Table 4.1 must be interpreted with care. First, America's population is more than four times that of Britain so it might be expected that American budgets for similar nationwide activity levels will be much higher. Second, this expectation will be, to some limited extent, offset by the proclivity, noted earlier, of associations in America to compete with one another to represent the same condition. And, third, the tendency of many American associations to operate devolved constitutions with local chapter funding excluded from national accounts (apart from chapter dues or subscriptions to the parent body) also reduces the ability to

Table 4.1 Patients' associations' expenditure, Britain and America, 1996–7

Turnover £	America		Britain	
	No.	*(%) (rounded)*	*No.*	*(%) (rounded)*
Under 25,000	12	(10)	40	(25)
25,000–100,000	34	(30)	39	(25)
100,000–250,000	16	(14)	24	(15)
250,000–1 million	27	(24)	21	(13)
1–5 million	16	(14)	22	(14)
Over 5 million	7	(6)	15	(9)
Totals	**112**		**161**	

An exchange rate US$1.5 = £1 has been used

make robust comparisons as relatively few British associations operate through office-based and large-scale branches of the type found in the case study of St Louis in Chapter 8. Autonomous branches of British associations with a turnover of £1000 or more now do have to register separately with the Charity Commission, but in the modest number of cases where this happens the amounts of expenditure found in this study were almost all very small.

Somewhat surprisingly the data in Table 4.1 indicate almost as many very small national associations in America as there are in Britain. It also indicates the vigour of associational life, with large numbers of modestly sized philanthropic organizations active in the social marketplace. Thus almost eighty British associations (50 per cent) had a turnover of less than £100,000. Many are in effect all-volunteer, but at the top end this is enough to fund a smallish office with a handful of paid staff. A typical instance of such an organization is the Miscarriage Association. In 1995–6 it spent £99,000. Half went on the salaries and office costs of the four staff, some part-time. It circulates a high quality quarterly newsletter, publishes a large number of leaflets, answered 18,000 queries in the year, supports 80 local groups, and has a 'good practice' information pack for health professionals and a database of 'expertise' for use by its 1300 members. Founded in 1981 by women who had had miscarriages, initially it was an all-volunteer association until 1987 when the Department of Health gave grant aid to the initial office costs.

Though slightly fewer American associations (40 per cent compared to 50 per cent in Britain) are in the 'small' category in having budgets of below £100,000, another 14 per cent fall into the next, or 'small-medium', category of a £100,000–250,000 turnover which, given the population difference, is no great sum to run an America-wide association. One at the lower end, with a £100,000 budget, is the National Spasmodic Torticollosis Association (a deformity of the neck, a neurological disorder). Founded in 1981 in Wisconsin, it had 2 paid staff at headquarters, 3400 members and 48 local chapters across the country. The National Marfan Foundation, also founded in 1981, had by 1996 grown to a near-£200,000 budget. It reported 11,000 members, 6 staff at its New York headquarters, and 35 state and local chapters. Interestingly, it compares quite closely in size with the Marfan Association UK, founded in 1984. This association employs 7 part-time staff in its Fleet, Hampshire offices, claims a membership of 1300 and lists 59 named local 'support networkers' as contact points. (A Dr Marfan first described this genetic connective tissue disorder affecting several organs in 1896; in 1990 a specific link to a gene was identified.)

The examples above, by focusing on small-scale organizations, may give a misleading impression that disease-related patients' associations are economically small beer. In aggregate this is far from the case. The main American study opens thus: 'Health charities are big business – a $10 billion business in 1990' (Bennett and Dilorenzo, 1994). This sum amounts to around 20 per cent of the total British spend on the whole of the NHS that year. In Table 4.1 there were 23 American and 37 British respondents with budgets in excess of £1 million. In 1996–7 those 37 British associations spent a massive £457 million, and the 161 respondents collectively comfortably topped £0.5 billion that year, or about the amount that the NHS spent per million of the population.

It must not be forgotten that patient-led and disease-specific criteria were used for inclusion in this study. To that sum of £0.5 billion can be added the spending of many health charities which, because their focus was solely on fund-raising for research, were not included. For example, the Imperial Cancer Research Fund alone has a research spend of over £50 million a year. It and the other 98 members of the Association of Medical Research Charities (32 of them included in this study) made a £420 million contribution to medical research in 1996–7 (Association of Medical Research Charities, 1997: 3). Hence a reasonable overall estimate is that British health charities operating on a national level have a turnover of around £1 billion. To that could be added the plethora of strictly local fund-raising activities which regularly provide equipment for almost all NHS hospitals. In Britain, as in America, health charities truly are big business, even if this is a highly fragmented and specialized 'industry'.

The theme of much of the study so far has been one of patients' associations experiencing growth. However, in Britain this trend suddenly received a severe jolting with the advent of the National Lottery in 1995, though in reality its arrival was just one further factor placing charities under financial pressure in the mid-1990s. In the rush by the public to buy lottery tickets at a rate of £70 million a week, direct giving to charities (of all categories, not just those in this study) was instantly affected. In many cases reserves were raided to maintain activity. 'It's been a tough year for fundraising' declared SENSE (The National Deafblind and Rubella Association) in its annual report (the main source for financial data for all the associations studied).

The Prader–Willi Syndrome Association was just one to quickly find itself in 'a precarious financial position', spending £20,000 more than its £72,000 income. And 'recession, market saturation and the National Lottery' made for 'a very challenging financial situation' declared the National Back Pain Association. The National Lottery's arrival did indeed coincide with both recession and increased competition as more and more charities were founded. The rapidly growing numbers of health charities alone, charted earlier in Table 3.1, is indicative of this, but other charitable sectors such as welfare, the environment, international aid and wildlife were also expanding, contributing to an increasingly crowded 'marketplace' within which an individual charity has to locate its niche. Falls of up to 20 per cent in donations in 1995–6 were reported by, among others, the Research Trust for Metabolic Diseases in Children, and REACH – Association for Children with Hand or Arm Deficiency. Retrenchment on a large scale was the fate of the Tourette Syndrome (UK) Association (its advisory and advocacy services, central to its activity, were 'temporarily suspended'), and by the Friedrich's Ataxia Group which had 'turned the corner' by 1997 only through unpaid trustees taking over several tasks from paid staff, allowing a move to cheaper premises, albeit in a location 'not ideal'.

For 37 of the British associations in this study, or more than one in five of respondents, the immediate villain was within a year or more to become something of a hero when the National Lottery Charities Board criteria were amended to allow it to begin to make grants to medical charities: these 37 made successful bids. Two others received considerable sums from Littlewood's scratch cards, introduced by the soccer pools company as a competitor to the National Lottery (which had badly affected its turnover). The 39 awards covered a huge variety of projects: holiday schemes, advocacy workers, awareness campaigns, networks of branches, more helplines, youth and ethnic minority activities, and, in three cases, the set-up costs of establishing a salaried national office. One of those three cases of financing an association's transition from all-volunteer to office-based was the Anaphylaxis Campaign (potentially fatal food allergies). The Campaign was founded only in 1994 (by the father of a child who died after eating some lemon meringue pie) but had grown to 4000 members by 1997 when a £58,933 Lottery grant enabled it 'to move up a gear'.

However, the divisive nature of this method of distributing monies to charities is also apparent. In their annual reports no fewer than one in eight respondents (22) openly admitted to having made a Lottery bid which failed (others may not have admitted this fact as annual reports naturally tend to focus on good news). The process was often strongly criticized. Completing the complex application forms had been a time-consuming task (so much so that one annual report admitted that the closing date had been missed). Frustration was widespread, and was further fuelled by news of the successes of others – unsuccessful associations often felt that their bids for similar schemes were at least as worthy of support.

The allocation of Lottery funds followed closely the general approach in recent years of Department of Health grants. Specific projects had to be put forward, and awards were for three years on the basis that this gave time for the project to establish itself and seek more secure income sources. There was a longish history of this working well: in all cases in this survey the projects had been maintained when the grant ended. Some 30 per cent (55) of responding associations had received Departmental grants in the 1990s, and many more referred to earlier awards.

As with the Lottery, the range of schemes supported by the Department of Health (DoH) has been enormous. Usually, though, the DoH more than the Lottery has been willing to fund basic office costs to allow all-volunteer associations experiencing growth to make the first big jump and set up a paid headquarters. About one-third of recipients reported that their DoH awards were for some form of office-based 'core' funding schemes. In the mid-1990s organizations such as the National Society for Phenylketonuria (an inherited biochemical abnormality controllable by diet), founded in 1973 by the parents of a child with the condition, and the National Association for the Relief of Paget's Disease (a chronic bone disorder), founded in 1973 by the wife of a sufferer who in 1983 received the OBE for her work, were supported in making this major transition. And the Prader–Willi Syndrome Association was helped out of its 'precarious' position through a grant to allow it to return to employing an administrative officer and to improve its very basic office premises in Derby. Thus smallish sums of money from the NHS budget were being used to recognize the rise of patient-led activity, and to encourage further development of patient self-help activity and, through that, of patient influence. Department of Health grants are an interesting example of active government sponsorship of groups who are quite likely to use their new-found strength to more effectively pressurize the donor.

This brief introduction to the finances of disease-related patients' associations has concentrated on their broad budgets and on some specific contributors to their incomes. A comprehensive analysis af the accounts of associations would identify further sources of income beyond direct charitable giving and, in Britain, Lottery awards and government grants. The larger associations, for example, often run trading services such as mail-order catalogues and high street shops. Perhaps more significant for the politics of health is the direct provision of care services, historically often preceding state involvement in health and welfare but today a mixture of charitable activity and of specific contracts with the state. This contractual relationship between the state and certain associations re-emerges in Chapter 6 in particular.

CONCLUSIONS

In Chapters 2–4 a clear picture of disease-related patients' associations has now been painted. The Anglo-American comparability of growth (of numbers, activities and finances) is most striking, not least because of the totally contrasting health care systems in the two countries. There are differences, caused by both geographical size and particular circumstances (such as the National Lottery), but the overall patterns are merely ruffled rather than fundamentally disturbed by these variables. The dominant scene is one of increased numbers and activity; of specialization and fragmentation; of some competition between groups; of enormous amounts of voluntary activity; of transitions from an all-volunteer to a salaried, office-based status; and of a sector of social policy which retains an image of philanthropy alongside levels of economic activity which, in aggregate, amount to 'big business'. In the next two chapters some significant consequences of this pattern are considered as the political economy and political effectiveness of disease-related patients' associations are placed under the spotlight.

5

THE POLITICAL ECONOMY OF PATIENTS' ASSOCIATIONS – EFFICIENCY AND EFFECTIVENESS

Growth – to the point where the label 'big business' has become an accurate description of disease-related patients' associations – does not in itself necessarily indicate that, collectively, they are either efficient or effective in pursuing their goals. In the next two chapters a number of activities common to many associations are examined. The choice of activities selected for scrutiny is designed to test the robustness of those goals in practice and the extent to which the public image of patients' associations as beneficial philanthropic organizations is justified.

In Chapter 4 it was noted that the associations studied here were founded to help 'relieve suffering' (to use the traditional Anglo-Saxon phraseology). This they sought and continue to seek to do in many different ways. Some concentrate on offering basic support, through everything from publishing regular and occasional literature to penpals, helplines, holiday schemes, local self-help groups, hardship grants, advocacy services and visitor projects. Some focus on fund-raising, commonly to support research into possible causes of diseases and new treatments, but sometimes to provide better immediate care facilities such as state-of-the-art technology or specialist pathology laboratories and outpatient clinics. A few are predominantly campaigning organizations. Most span two or all three of these roles, though many – and almost all of the newer ones who constitute the vast majority of patients' associations, founded since the mid-1970s – began life stimulated by the desire to improve support for individual patients and to encourage self-help. Almost all share another important set of attributes too: enthusiasm, selfless commitment, huge amounts of drive and energy, and a determination to triumph over adversity. They are widely perceived as representing the 'voluntary sector' at its best.

Dangers and pitfalls face patients' associations. Oddly, many of these stem directly from the very attributes that are also their strength. As health charities they are widely perceived to be valuable philanthropic organizations: that is their image, and their ambition. Goodwill and trust abound, both within them and in terms of the public's perception of them. They do 'good work', surely? Indeed they do, and some of that work was explored briefly in Chapter 4 and recapped above. The basic question to be examined now is whether they could be even more effective. In exploring this there will be both actual and implied criticism of their overall performance. That cannot be avoided, but it in no way challenges their importance as key actors in the drive for improvements in the quality of life of millions of people who live with unfortunate and often unpleasant medical conditions.

Chapter 5 selects activities which focus on the political economy and organizational attributes of patients' associations. It briefly considers their record of financial probity before utilizing their published accounts to assess financial efficiency. The 'in whose interests?' issue is then analysed by reviewing the extent to which associations may be 'colonized' by the interests of health care providers and producers rather than being truly patient-led. Finally some consequences of the organizational culture labelled in America as 'turfism' (associations working independently from, and competing with, one another) are identified, partly through case studies of recent attempts in Britain to form alliances and coalitions. This leads directly onto Chapter 6, which concentrates on their political effectiveness as influencers of health care service provision.

PROBITY: FINANCIAL IRREGULARITIES

Wherever there is money there is the potential for fraud. Excessive levels of trust and goodwill within an organization enhance the opportunities for abuse. Though happily rare, there have been 'periodic instances of outright fraud' (Ware 1989: 28) and in Britain in the early 1990s the media produced much 'publicity surrounding scandals relating to Humana, the British Legion and SCOPE (formerly the Spastics Society)' (Kendall and Knapp 1996: 4). This is despite the fact that the receipt of charity status appears dependent on and to be accompanied by fairly stringent rules about audit arrangements, though policing of those rules has been patchy in both countries. In Britain, for example, a 1987 National Audit Office report found that the very basic requirement to submit annual accounts to the Charity Commission was being met by only about 40 per cent of charities, and that only 13 of the 330 Charity Commission staff were involved in 'investigations, including enquiries from the press' (Ware 1989: 205, 208).

The 1987 report was highly critical of the Charity Commission, indicating that its regulatory role was being performed inadequately. There has been some tightening up since then, including new audit rules in 1995, and a new requirement on local branches with a turnover of £1000 or more to register with the Commission separately from their parent body. Although some of the smallest associations choose not to seek charity status because their turnover is too small to make it worthwhile to gain the resultant tax advantages, they are financially pretty insignificant and any fraud they experienced would necessarily involve trivial amounts. The new rules have not fully succeeded: some 20 per cent of the largest (with salaried staff and therefore presumably the most professionally organized) British charities failed to meet the deadline in 1998–9 for submitting their accounts to the Commission (no data were released on the overall percentage missing the deadline but it doubtless remains high).

In both Britain and America there have been a handful of publicized health charity frauds in the past decade. Rapid changes of executive director in two St Louis chapters were reported at interviews, with a surrounding atmosphere implying at the very least mismanagement, if not outright fraud. But these cases pale into insignificance alongside the dramatic United Way 1992 scandal which 'shocked the nation' and exposed the weaknesses of the American charity watchdogs (Bennett and Dilorenzo 1994: x–xi, ch. 3). United Way is a federated fund-raising scheme through payroll deductions in participating companies, with the proceeds then distributed to charities recognized by the local United Way trustees (see Ware 1989: 131–5 for details). The resignation of its national president came amidst coast-to-coast media allegations of perks, patronage and sexual misdeeds. A second fraud case in the mid-1990s involved the embezzlement of up to US$1 million by, and the resulting imprisonment of, the executive director of the Parkinson's Disease Association. This too shocked the charity community, though it received rather less media coverage, maybe because sexual activity was not an issue.

Perhaps because of the tightening up of charity regulation following the 1987 National Audit Office criticisms, British examples of fraud in the past decade have been almost non-existent. And they have not involved the organizations studied here. This does not mean that patients' associations are now exempt from the dangers of financial and organizational misconduct. Indeed, the 1997 postal survey revealed the case of the Diabetes Foundation, with an 'interim manager' from a large firm of chartered accountants in post. This appointment had been made not by the Foundation's trustees or management committee but by the Charity Commission, following concerns about the legal and financial situation, including missing accounts. The existing trustees had become almost defunct and the 1982-founded organization was in effect moribund though with, in this case, no apparent fraud or embezzlement of funds. In other cases, changes of chief and senior officers were reported without the usual accompaniment of public praise and thanks in annual reports, which suggests a level of incompetence if not impropriety.

FINANCIAL EFFICIENCY: HIGH-COST CHARITIES

Fraud is a criminal offence; excessive spending is not – but it is possibly a greater danger facing charities in that it can happen more easily, and for apparently perfectly proper motives. The health of the political economy of patients' associations is here measured through analysing the level of expenditure on what are commonly labelled as overheads. These are defined in this study as spending under the two headings of central administration/management and of fund-raising costs. Examples of seemingly high overheads appear to be far from rare.

In 1972 it emerged that the 'unpaid' president of the (American) National Foundation for Infant Paralysis had actually drawn a salary of US$100,000 plus a further US$70,000 in expenses. Of the 28 board members (unpaid part-timers, as is the norm) only three knew that he was getting paid, though even they were unaware of the amount (Bakal 1979: 143). No law had been broken, but the case dramatically illustrates a common weakness: board membership of a charity is often made up of supporters rather than sceptics, and boards consequently operate through a great deal of trust and goodwill. With self-regulation potentially weak, the onus falls on external watchdogs to uncover and report financial mismanagement, and that does not always work.

Boards and external regulators have no precise formula, or even generally accepted benchmarks for assessing what constitutes high costs. Some economists have in the past offered tentative criteria. The main recent American study, for example, criticized the American Cancer Society and the American Lung Association for spending 39 per cent and 42.5 per cent, respectively, on 'staff compensation'. Using charities' own accounts, the authors went on to allege that among ten state divisions of the American Cancer Society investigated, direct services provided by the Society accounted for only between 8.6 and 22.5 per cent of spending (Bennett and Dilorenzo 1994: 72–80). To be fair to the Society, this overlooked the fact that one of its key objectives is to raise funds for research (US$32.9 million in 1989) and so service provision was but part of its total activity.

This study examined a range of patients' association accounts in both Britain and America before establishing an apparently reasonable target for 'overheads'. The examination indicated that around 25 per cent of turnover on 'overheads' normally represented an acceptable benchmark at the upper end. Among exemplars which contributed to this judgement were the St Louis chapter of the Juvenile Diabetes Foundation International (JDF). JDF's executive director described its 'whole mission' as being to raise funds for research. The three paid staff in (by British standards) fairly palatial offices meant that it was spending just about 25 per cent of its 1996–7 income of US$476,000 on administrative and fund-raising costs. This single example was closely in line with, though at the top end of, other St Louis chapters, according to data analysed by the executive director of the Combined Health Appeal of Greater St Louis (a fifteen-member coalition of associations established from non-recipients of United Way support, though since 1988 the two now work together on the main United Way annual appeal). He had scrutinized the accounts of all fifteen to try to establish and recommend guidelines of good management practice.

Further support for the selection of the 25 per cent benchmark is in British data. The Hodgkin's Disease and Lymphoma Association (HDLA) offers a good illustration. Founded in 1986, it grew in its first decade to include about 6000 'members and supporters', with a network of local groups, an office with salaried staff from 1994, and a 1996–7 income (£310,000) which places it right in the middle of patients' associations in terms of financial turnover (as seen in Table 4.1 above). In the 1996–7 annual report the treasurer of HDLA publicly apologized for spending as much as 27 per cent of funds raised on overheads. He went on to announce an expectation that this would fall, hopefully through better income generation rather than staff cuts – indeed it had to fall, he stated, if the Association were to be cost-effective.

Though established by a combination of both evidence and judgement, a 25 per cent benchmark for overheads thus seems to be a reasonable rule-of-the-thumb target against which to review activity. It was created in the absence of published 'league tables' of charity costs. It is important to understand that the whole concept of a benchmark is designed solely to raise questions when outliers emerge. There will be good reasons why some associations appear to run at lower cost levels, and why others have higher overheads – though annual reports and accounts only rarely comment on those reasons.

The American survey revealed more cases of high overheads than those of the Cancer and Lung Associations, cited above. The Muscular Dystrophy Association, for example, had a US$105 million turnover in 1996–7 and spent US$7.3 million on 'management and general' costs but an enormous US$20.2 million on fundraising, giving an 'overhead ratio' of 26 per cent. However, it has to be said immediately that in Britain the use of the 25 per cent benchmark gives rise to a much higher number of apparent 'outliers' than does the American data. It is straightaway noticeable, for example, that the British Juvenile Diabetes Foundation had overheads in 1996–7 of 35 per cent or £156,000 (of which £80,000 went on pay and national insurance contributions of its four staff) out of a total spend of £448,000. Above, its sister organization in St Louis recorded just 25 per cent and was an exemplar of that benchmark level. Using the annual accounts provided by the postal survey, at least 22 of the 170 British respondents showed overheads of above 25 per cent. If the tiny all-volunteer associations with no proper offices or salary costs are excluded (in Table 4.1 they accounted for one association in four), this actually means that almost one-fifth of office-based patients' associations in Britain spent more than 25 per cent of turnover on overheads.

Any criticism of cost-effectiveness must necessarily be made only very cautiously and tentatively. Before rushing to judgement it is important to recognize that in Britain the standard charity accounts have two potential weaknesses which make it important to interpret them with care. First, they may not always represent an accurate allocation of costs. Senior officers, for example, may be involved in a range of activities which go beyond the usual label of 'management and administration', but their salaries may not be apportioned accordingly unless they keep a diary of their work – as was being recommended to its members by the St Louis Combined Health Appeal following a detailed analysis of the executive director's own time. They may, for instance, spend some time with helpline counselling or make public awareness speeches or write educational leaflets. Second, in British charity accounts the two standard headings used here to calculate overheads are 'management and administration', which is quite clear but is subject to the problem outlined above, and 'fund-raising and publicity', which is less than satisfactory as it can include a myriad of costs not directly connected with the fund-raising process and hence not truly overheads. The Multiple Sclerosis Society, for example, had spent £247,000 on a 'public awareness campaign' in 1995, those costs appearing under this heading.

Bearing these points in mind, the examples below of seemingly high levels of overheads in the 1995–7 financial years are deliberately not listed in order of scale as this would wrongly imply that a robust league table can be constructed. Those with overheads above the 25 per cent benchmark included the Stillbirth and Neonatal Death Society (SANDS) with nine staff at headquarters and 45 per cent of its £418,000 income coming under the two relevant headings in their accounts; the Research Trust for Metabolic Diseases in Children with 35 per cent of its £330,000 income going on its overheads; the Cystic Fibrosis Trust, spending 30 per cent of its £4.8 million income in that way (or 35 per cent if income from investments is ignored); the Toxoplasmosis Trust (a parasitic infection) which raised £95,000 in donations but spent £30,000 on fundraising and publicity, and a further £38,000 on management and administration, making overheads account for no less than 55 per cent of total income; and the Spinal Injuries Association with a £1.1 million income but £468,000 overheads.

A league table restricted to fund-raising costs alone would also have outliers. The Stroke Association raised donations of £1.9 million but recorded fund-raising and publicity costs of £903,000 in so doing. Other instances included the Parkinson's Disease Society which raised £1.5 million but spent £474,000 on fund-raising costs;

while the Motor Neurone Disease Association, in 'a difficult year for the Team', had the unfortunate experience of spending an extra £95,000 on fund-raising to bring in additional donations of only £142,000.

The apparently highest overheads in this survey came from the Dystonia Society (a neurological movement disorder) with a 1996–7 income and expenditure of about £230,000 of which over 75 per cent went on the two relevant headings. Because its constitution gives the 30 local groups autonomy that the national accounts may not fully reflect the total picture. Other apparent outliers include the Ileostomy and Internal Pouch Support Group, with a total budget of £301,000 of which over half (£155,000) was on its overheads; the Miscarriage Association which spent £50,000 of its £99,000 income on salaries and office costs (despite an annual report which repeatedly emphasized the important roles played by volunteers in supporting the four salaried officials); and Baby Life Support Systems (BLISS) which spent £325,000 (or £390,000 if the administrative costs of its 'Give As You Earn' scheme are included) of its £1 million income on its overheads. The BLISS 1996–7 accounts interestingly included a claim by the executive director that it is a 'prudent and cost-effective' organization with low overheads.

Much too rarely does an association acknowledge that there might be a need to accompany its accounts with some explanation of the specific (to that charity) financial picture which is presented in the raw figures. In contrast, concerns about general factors like the National Lottery and the impact of recession abound, as indicated in Chapter 4; so do claims of cost-effective administration, as with BLISS above. The Hodgkin's Disease and Lymphoma Association's concern about its 27 per cent overheads, cited above, was a rare instance of a self-critical report. MIND (National Association for Mental Health) was another exception. It admitted that fund-raising costs of £895,000 in 1996–7 'are significant' in that donations raised were slightly less than double that sum (£1.76 million). This was, it explained, because of its high 'individual donor base' in contrast to those charities which benefit from sizeable corporate contributions.

In other cases there were signs of concern elsewhere in the literature, usually in the report of the chief executive. Organizational reviews to improve the general performance of an association were frequently mentioned, and some retrenchment of services and activities occasionally arose. This latter was unusual and the whole tone of annual reports is understandably optimistic and upbeat, given that they are the public showpiece of the association, designed to boost the morale of officials, volunteers, donors and potential supporters. Nevertheless, Breast Cancer Care was one to admit to being under severe pressure as the support it had received from Macmillan Cancer Relief since 1981 was about to be phased out and new staff had been appointed to generate an increase in donations. Overheads thus rose by 67 per cent in one year, accounting for some 30 per cent of expenditure as a result, despite income rising by 46 per cent, and by 166 per cent over two years.

Others reorganizing to reflect the financial pressures of the mid-1990s included the Multiple Sclerosis Society. In 1996 it cut £95,000 from its £411,000 management costs. The impact of this on its ratio of overheads to income was, however, offset by a reduction in income because fund-raising expenses (of £1.9 million) rose to 32 per cent of donations. The Friedrich's Ataxia Group was another to retrench, from 33 per cent to 25 per cent in overheads through reducing the payroll by £34,000 and relying more on volunteer workers. And the Muscular Dystrophy Group was reported (by an 'affiliated' society also in the survey) as having made five family care workers redundant. The affiliate commented 'we are truly sorry that the service has been depleted'.

The emphasis so far has been on apparently high costs. At the other end of the scale there is an equal dearth of published 'league tables' of the most economical, with overhead ratios well below the 25 per cent benchmark. If there were then, in Britain, the National Osteoporosis Society (income £1.45 million, with under 10 per cent spent on overheads); the Reynaud's and Scleroderma Association (income £537,000, overheads under 15 per cent); and the National Association for Colitis and Crohn's Disease (income £848,000, overheads £58,000 or only 7 per cent) would be leading contenders for top place. All three were founded in the 1979–86 period and all have grown rapidly from tiny beginnings, seemingly in a very cost-effective manner.

In direction comparison with American data, the accounts of this last group indicate overheads almost exactly in line with the 8–10 per cent found at the lower end of costs in St Louis in the Combined Health Appeal's analysis, cited earlier (page 73). The contrast in Britain is so sharp with the previous high-cost examples that there appears to be ample scope for the external watchdogs of charities to develop 'best practice' guidelines. True, charities vary greatly: some find fund-raising relatively easy because the cause they represent impacts widely on the public's mind; the types of services they offer differ; the work of headquarters staff is dissimilar; and the relationships with local branches can be constitutionally and financially contrasting.

Nevertheless, this study suggests that there is a strong case for examining these and other differences to establish public confidence in the cost-effectiveness of all health charities, and to ensure that adequate explanations accompany some of the apparently high costs. Precisely the same thing is true in America, where the charity watchdogs have also been generally ineffective. Large sums spent on fund-raising in particular need to be justified. Many donors would not be impressed to hear that in certain cases up to half their donation went on fund-raising costs, and that very substantial sums, millions of pounds in the case of the largest charities, were expended in this manner.

IN WHOSE INTERESTS? AUTONOMY AND PROFESSIONAL COLONIZATION

Getting the balance right between working *with* health professionals and working *for* them is another difficult area for disease-related patients' associations. They were founded and exist to work in the interests of, and to support people with, the particular medical condition they represent, seeking improved treatment and care. Inevitably one potential strategy involves working closely with 'the experts': those who, in one way or another, work to provide health care. Indeed, many of the associations studied here were founded by a combination of patients and providers, and a few by providers alone. Thus 'rheumatologists, physiotherapists and patients at the Royal National Hospital, Bath' initiated the National Ankylosing Spondylitis Society in 1976 (Williams 1989: 143). Furthermore, most have panels of medical or scientific advisers and several have commercial sponsorship and other financial relationships with the suppliers of goods and equipment.

In principle, and in most cases, this makes good sense. Influencing provision and resource allocation through 'insider' status and channels of access has long been recognized by social scientists as an important attribute of the most successful pressure groups (Baggott 1995: 18–20, for example) and there is no reason to believe that this conventional analysis is inapplicable in principle to patients' associations. There is a practical danger about its unquestioning acceptance, however. Patients have traditionally been seen as fairly powerless customers, weak in the face of the professionalism and mystique of the medical profession, and of management interests (Alford 1975: ch. 5, for example). In those circumstances any relationship will not easily be one of equals, and there is a potential danger that too close a relationship will result in the association becoming subservient to the interests of the providers of care. If what is here termed 'professional colonization' occurs, patient and member needs become secondary and are not the key to understanding associations' activities and influence.

Three groups of interests can be separated, each with an incentive to 'colonize' associations. First, the medical profession (divisible into subcategories of practising doctors and of research scientists) has obvious interests in encouraging the supply of extra patients and research monies, and associations have historically offered both through working for provider recognition of 'new' illnesses and diseases, and through fund-raising. Second, the suppliers of health technology have equally obvious interests both collectively, in encouraging demand for their products (from drugs to body scanners and to home aids like bags and other stoma care products and specialist chairs or mobility equipment), and individually, in pushing their particular product as better than that offered by competitors. And, third, there are the corporate payers and providers of health care. Here interests vary, with payers like the NHS in Britain and governments and insurance companies in America anxious about cost control and containment, but hospitals (in both countries) interested in enhancing demand for their services. That all three groups have sought to colonize some associations is inevitable, given their interests. That all three have had some success is apparent: there is a very real danger of some associations being, in effect, subverted.

The recognition of Alzheimer's disease and its consequences offers a good example of medical interests in action. Until the late 1970s this was a medical condition which remained officially unrecognized, though geriatricians and carers were increasingly aware of evidence about mood swings and memory failures which did not fit into conventional diagnoses. In America a tripartite alliance of scientific researchers, the National Institute on Ageing and the newly formed (in 1980) patients' (or carers, in reality) association 'elevated the disease from one perceived as dreadful but insignificant, to one which was accepted as socially and medically significant, and a leading cause of death' (Fox 1989, see Walt 1994: 115).

One consequence of increased public awareness and concern was 'an increase in research funds made available for the disease', not least through the efforts of the Alzheimer's Association both in lobbying for governmental aid and in fund-raising. The history was similar in Britain and today its Alzheimer's Disease Society (founded in 1979, a year before the American association) directly funds research fellowships and projects, spending close to £500,000 a year on this activity alone.

In this case there is no evidence of any obvious conflict of interest between patients and colonizers. The associations and the doctors were pursuing a similar agenda, though that fact alone is insufficient to show that all is well. There are, however, several other instances where an apparent similarity of objectives masks what is in effect colonization by vested interests within medicine. Take the example of the American Cancer Society and the funding of research as a good illustration of what can happen. In 1976 (perhaps for obvious reasons the last year in which the annual report gave such exact data) no less than 88.6 per cent of its grants were awarded to projects at institutions with which board members were affiliated (Bennett and Dilorenzo 1994: 162). Even in America the world of medical research is a smallish community, and there is no allegation of impropriety made by the authors reporting this. They go on to suggest that the proportion had probably fallen to below 40 per cent by 1990. Their concerns centre less on the issue of conflicts of interest than on the nature of the research: they argue that colonization might result in potentially exciting projects leading to medical breakthroughs not getting funded because they were the ideas of 'outsiders' who were not part of the medical establishment.

Strict peer review systems, demanded as a condition of membership of the (British) Association of Medical Research Charities because it is 'essential in maintaining credibility', should allay those fears. There is no equivalent American organization to AMRC, which has existed as a 'trade association' informally since 1972 but which was relaunched in 1987 as a formal organization 'to further medical research . . . (and) . . . to advance the effectiveness of those charities of which a principal activity is medical research' (AMRC 1997: 3). Its 99 members in 1996–7 funded some £420 million of research, over three-quarters of this being from the largest four (Wellcome Trust £195 million; Imperial Cancer Research Fund £52 million; Cancer Research Campaign £42 million; British Heart Foundation £34 million). The vast majority of associations in this study are not AMRC members, often because research funding is a relatively minor part of their activities.

Despite the AMRC's lead to the charity sector on peer review, there remains some evidence of a closeness of relationships between doctors and associations which does raise questions about the autonomy of certain organizations in this study. The chair of the 28-strong panel of Medical Advisers of the British Retinitis Pigmentosa Society (a hereditary incurable degeneration of the retina), for example, is a professor at St Thomas' Hospital (a prestigious London teaching hospital). In 1996, the Society applied successfully to the National Lottery board for a £69,000 grant to support a specialist laboratory at St Thomas' Hospital. British Sjogren's Syndrome Association (an auto-immune rheumatic disease peculiar to women) was founded in 1987 by a patient as a self-help group but by 1997 every one of its fourteen-member council had professional qualifications. The three trustees of the National Association for the Relief of Paget's Disease, founded in 1973 by the wife of a sufferer, are all doctors: two are also chair and vice-chair, another doctor is honorary secretary and these four are a majority of the six-member Scientific Advisory Committee. The 'research director' of Foresight (Association for the Promotion of Pre-conceptual Care) is from Surrey University. Over half the Association's small special fund, a sum of £20,000, went to Surrey University in 1996–7. Activities at Bath Rheumatic Hospital featured heavily in the National Ankylosing Spondylitis Society 1995–6 annual report: founded there in 1976, the chair is still from that hospital.

In similar vein, two of the four new research awards made in 1996 by the Psoriasis Association went to research committee members or advisers. Five of the fourteen advisers to the Raynaud's and Scleroderma Association were running projects which, between them, accounted for about 70 per cent of the £600,000 worth of projects being supported, and three of these projects will have received £1.3 million by the year 2001. The Vitiligo Society supports three research projects with tiny sums of money: two of them are run by leading members (the secretary (a doctor) and one of the eight on its medical advisory panel). Its offices are located at the headquarters of the British Association of Dermatologists, the relevant professional body. The Progressive Supranuclear Palsy Association (PSPA) is truly patient-led, having been founded only in 1994 by a husband and his late wife (who died from it in 1995). The husband has put enormous energy into building up an international society, even building offices over his garage, and has recruited well known names as active supporters. PSPA's policy of calling for centres of excellence for a pretty rare condition is understandable even though it raises questions of geographical access to care. Three specialist clinics are established or envisaged: in London, Cambridge and possibly Liverpool. The two clinical research fellows that PSPA sponsors are based in London and Cambridge, the former working under the overall direction of the chairman of its medical advisory panel.

The final example of relations between the medical profession and patients' associations in Britain is slightly different but again illustrates the scope for medical influence and colonization. The British Liver Trust has objectives listed as 'to provide support and information to people affected by liver disease and to fund research' (Association of Medical Research Charities 1997: 32) which it does through a glossy newsletter, a helpline, leaflets and 13 local support groups. It thus has all the hallmarks of an active, successful patients' association, but it is also something of a 'front' organization, having been founded in 1988 by liver specialists. Considerable sums are spent on running prestigious conferences for specialists and the Trust launched a major appeal for £5 million to spend on research in specialist laboratories. It reports a membership of only 750 patients, but its mailing list runs to 24,000 names.

It is important to reiterate that there is no suggestion of illegality or malpractice by anyone in any of the above examples, and doctors active in associations normally are unpaid for their work. The instances are cited simply to make the point that patients' associations which, naturally and understandably, forge relationships with doctors do face problems of trying simultaneously to work with the 'experts' and to retain their autonomy as consumer bodies. Interests can be in some conflict, and associations can be unduly influenced. Most of the time there is no danger of different interests and agendas being pursued; some of the time there is. One of the commonest difficulties lies in the ability to establish genuine and independent peer review of research proposals in the tight-knit field of often highly specialized medical research with only a handful of scientists interested in the rare conditions which many patients' associations represent. Another is the possibility that promising but unorthodox lines of research may miss out on charity funding unless the researchers are on the inside track. And, finally, the coordinating mechanisms for research funding are rather 'hit-and-miss' in Britain, arguably more so than in America where the National Institutes of Health play significant roles. The National Cancer Institute, for example, has no robust equivalent in Britain, where a coordinating committee resourced by the three major fund-raisers lacks teeth.

The second group of interests was identified as the suppliers of health technology. Of these the pharmaceutical industry funds almost half the £250 million spent on cancer research each year in Britain, and a similar amount comes from the 13 cancer charities which are members of the Association of Medical Research Charities. However, for this study, wider interests than research alone create the potential for drug and equipment company colonization of patients' associations. These centre on patients as direct and indirect (through prescriptions) purchasers of company products. Advertisments in association newsletters and other literature are commonplace. Money changes hands both through these and through outright donations. The biggest danger facing associations here is that, whatever they say in the small print of their publications, they can give the appearance of endorsing products. Worse: they may even be influenced into positive reporting of new products, or the reverse of failing to report negatively on product performance.

Dependence on drug company finances can become excessive. In Britain the Primary Immunodeficiency Association, for example, had reached a position in 1995 where no less than 60 per cent of its income was from the pharmaceutical industry. This was dramatically reduced by increasing its fund-raising and obtaining more grants in 1996. The Vitiligo Society was one of several using drug companies to sponsor its literature, part of which advised members 'to be cautious [about] alleged complementary remedies'. The Society is one of many skin disease associations, all of which operate in a market of enormous competition between drug companies.

That skin disease, diet-related and other similar associations with members dependent on purchases of health technology have to be particularly careful is shown by the case of the (UK) Acne Support Group (ASG). Chaired by a medical specialist at Hammersmith Hospital, ASG ran into public criticism in 1998. It was openly collaborating with no less than 14 drug companies in trying to raise public awareness, giving new members a 'goodie bag' of their products. One drug company offered an 'unrestricted grant' to it for the creation of a web site. Some 25–35 per cent of its income was from other drug companies. Controversy arose when it was revealed in the press that two of the largest donations (actually pretty small sums of money) had come from the manufacturers of two drugs where alarming side-effects had been reported (Minocin, where up to 150 patients were said to be considering legal action owing to literally crippling alleged side-effects; and Roaccutane, connected in the media as a possible contributor to a teenage suicide). Media criticism was that the ASG was disinclined in its literature to give strong warnings to would-be users of these drugs because of the financial relationship. Whether or not this was entirely fair (the snapshot sample of literature received as part of the 1997 survey did not contain such warnings), it illustrates the dangers of colonization and conflicts of interest.

Also in Britain, the Urostomy Association acknowledged receiving funds from 'the appliance industry [and] its sister organisations' both as donations and through advertisements: its journal (newsletter) is a 72-page glossy product, ably edited by a volunteer but packed with adverts from both manufacturers and home delivery suppliers. The Psoriasis Association's shorter but similarly glossy newsletter not only includes drug adverts but also has articles about new drugs written by manufacturers who sign up as 'corporate members' (all the proper disclaimers are there but so is the resultant publicity). Pharmaceutical companies marketing two potentially very significant new drugs made donations to the National Association for the Relief of Paget's Disease (NARPD) in 1995–6: in the case of one of them, Skelid, the manufacturers Sanofi, funded posters publicizing the association including the key claim about Skelid and Paget's Disease: 'the fact . . . now treatable'. A prominent Dutch drug company sponsored the 1996–7 annual Conference of the Association for Glycogen Storage Disease, flying in an American researcher sponsored by another, American, drug company. And so on. Posters, advertisements, sponsorship and other forms of supplier colonization abound.

Again, everything above is legal, but associations need to be well aware of the dangers that they can face in appearing to offer product endorsement as a consequence of bolstering their finances by accepting the support of the health technology industry. The Child Growth Foundation was one to be publicly wary of 'drug company capture', while the Herpes Virus Association's (HVA) policy states: 'we value our independence, particularly since patient groups for herpes simplex in other countries are funded and inevitably influenced by a drug company'. About to lose 35 per cent of its income by the withdrawal of London Boroughs' Grants Committee funding, HVA was striving to bridge the gap without approaching the pharmaceutical industry. The third set of interests offering some danger of colonization was that of the corporate and governmental institutions paying for and providing health care. Hospitals can host associations as in the cases of the St Louis chapters of the American Parkinson Disease Association and the Leukemia Society of America: philanthropic gestures which potentially bring patients to them, particularly when adjacent specialist clinics are offered.

The Schizophrenia Association of Great Britain was, from its 1970 foundation until 1990, a part of the University of Bangor in Wales. There are close links with hospitals in the cases of the Purine Metabolic Patients' Association (the AGM was at Guy's Hospital, London, where the association supports a specialist laboratory), and the British Thyroid Foundation, 'founded in 1992 by a sufferer', and now housed in a Leeds hospital though also associated with the British Thyroid Association, a professional body.

A quite different form of colonization also exists in relationships in Britain between associations and the NHS. The history of many older charities includes what is now seen as mainstream service provision, to fill some of the gaps in the pre-welfare state era. Today parts of that activity continue on a properly funded basis, with several patients' associations having contracts with NHS payers to act as providers. Examples include the Stroke Association with a £2 million contract which ran at a loss of £300,000 in 1996–7. In America there are similar contractual arrangements with payers. These are in essence commercial transactions, and they may involve retendering against competition from time to time. A particular difficulty arises from the blurred boundary between mainstream, properly funded service provision and supplementary unfunded charitable activity which could today be construed as mainstream. Patient education and support services might fall into this category, including helplines and support groups. In such cases payers like the NHS, or the Medicare and Medicaid authorities in America, are, in effect, containing their costs by relying on philanthropy to provide services which, if they were to fold, would have to continue to be provided. This is a form of colonization by abstinence.

A good illustration of colonization by abstinence lies in the main work in Britain of Baby Life Support Systems (BLISS), which is raising funds to provide equipment to hospital special care baby units. In 1996–7 as many as 52 NHS hospitals shared £470,000 worth of that equipment. These numbers indicate both that BLISS is not

restricting its support to highly specialized, state-of-the-art technology of the type only to be found in the most prestigious of hospitals, and that massively expensive technology is not involved.
Arguably the NHS should be funding what amounts to routine,
mainstream equipment. A parallel example is that of the Headway
National Head Injuries Association which provides 40 Headway
House day care centres. Their location was unplanned, raising issues
about equality of access (the key founding principle of the NHS).
Facilities vary enormously, some being properly housed in hospitals
while others are in church halls (raising issues of quality and equity).

Other instances of associations providing arguably mainstream
health care include the Tuberous Sclerosis Society, which has
helped establish five specialist clinics. It pays for them too.
Although the Society views this activity as 'excellent value for
money', it is debatable whether the estimated 7000 with this complex genetic disorder should have to rely on charity funding. Similarly the UK Thalassaemia Society, by no stretch of the imagination
a wealthy charity, had to spend £16,000 'to keep the laboratory
open at University College Hospital [London] which would have
closed due to lack of [NHS] funds', while the comparatively
affluent British Heart Foundation, which 'receives no government
funding' is funding around two-thirds of Britain's cardiovascular
research, into a condition which successive 1990s governments have
seen as a top priority for action to reduce death rates, with targets
set for the NHS to meet in both the 1992 and 1998 public health
policy statements. State support for research funding remains at a
far lower level in Britain than in America. There associations regularly produce league tables of support by disease as part of their
political activity (see Chapter 6).

EXCESSIVE AUTONOMY: TURFISM?

In Chapter 3 the fragmentation of disease-related patients' associations was charted, and the existence of what can be termed 'competing groups' was established. Examples from both Britain and
America, each of them pluralist, capitalist liberal democracies, suggested that this feature of associations was understandable but that
there were costs including administrative duplication, higher overheads, and possibly of a certain amount of wasted energy by volunteers.

American attempts to coordinate to improve cost-effectiveness have so far been rare and have in essence been a failure. United Way has never seen itself as having this role, and the newer Combined Health Appeal, now active in forty of the largest metropolitan areas, is still feeling its way. The scope for sharing the most basic of facilities – office space, printing and computing technology, reception and administrative staff – alone is enormous, given the American style of operating chapters through paid executive directors often operating out of tiny office suites with just one or two assistants. Although the St Louis Combined Health Appeal (CHA) recognized this, its attempts to facilitate joint action, discussed in Chapter 8, have yet to impact on the deep-seated culture of autonomy. Indeed, in offering support and meeting facilities to the few remaining all-volunteer chapters, the CHA may actually encourage the birth of more separate office-based salaried chapters as this remains a common ambition.

Coordination initiatives in Britain have had a different emphasis, on policy goals rather than administrative efficiency. In particular there have been attempts at improving access to policy makers through joint campaigning (the word here has a low-key meaning). This is examined in Chapter 6 because of its significance as a political activity whereas the focus here is on general cost-effectiveness. Meanwhile all the 220 or so associations identified continue to operate autonomously, with the single exception of the Association of Cystic Fibrosis Adults, which is part of (and solely funded by) another health charity, the Cystic Fibrosis Trust. A handful of other collaborative managerial relationships did also emerge from the survey. These included arrangements made by Charcot–Marie–Tooth International (UK) (a hereditary, progressive but non-fatal neurological genetic defect) for the Muscular Dystrophy Group to disburse the (modest) funds raised for research. As noted in Chapter 3, this culture of autonomy includes the voluntary provision of offices in private homes, sometimes through building or converting premises. It means that headquarters are scattered throughout Britain, and that potentially overlapping organizations often have no contact with one another.

Some of this competition is entirely understandable in that it is a consequence of different beliefs or principles about medical conditions and treatment systems. Mottoes or soundbites alone often reveal these differences. In Britain, for example, Hearing Concern claims to be 'the only national charity [centring on] the needs of hard-of-hearing people using speech as their main means of communication'. The four main charities in this area have very divided views about the merits of sign language, cochlear implants and other approaches.

Divided views are equally apparent in the field of mental illness. MIND (National Association for Mental Health) has long campaigned for more and better 'care in the community', a policy which has received bad publicity in recent years through a series of major incidents, many resulting in citizen deaths. One of MIND's competitors, SANE (Schizophrenia – A National Emergency), has been pressing for improved inpatient facilities, with some apparent political success. Within mental illness, competing mottoes or jingles in the search for support also include the Manic Depression Fellowship's 'largest user-led self-help organization in the field of mental health' and Depression Alliance's 'now the leading organization helping sufferers and carers'. Manic Depression Fellowship's claim of user-led self-help is one perceived by others as an attractive feature. The National Kidney Federation, to give just one of many possible examples, projects the image that it is 'the only national organization run by kidney patients for the benefit of kidney patients'.

In other areas of disease and illness, competition seems not to be based on principles. American and British interviews threw up numerous comments of the order of 'they are not on speaking terms' or even 'they loathe each other'. 'They' here refers to whole associations, but doubtless individual officials and active volunteers quickly acquire the culture. The St Louis chapter's executive director of the Asthma and Allergy Foundation reported being told on appointment to 'compete with the American Lung Association'. Each association works to carve out its niche in the charity sector or market, if necessarily at the expense of competitors with shared or overlapping interests. Though competition is in many ways a sign of a healthy and energetic sector of society and the economy in both countries, this activity is not always either cost-effective or disease-effective. Two instances suffice to illustrate this, one from each country.

In Britain the neurological disease ME (myalgic encephalomyelitis) – now often referred to as chronic fatigue syndrome – has spawned competing associations. The ME Association, founded in 1976, is a little larger than the 1987 Action for ME although the advent of the latter caused the former to experience some decline. Competition for membership has been strong. In 1996, the ME Association again claimed it was 'now the largest', though local groups had reduced from over 150 in 1991 to about 100, and membership of 'about 9000' compares with the 1989 claim of 12,000. Action for ME claims to be different in principle in favouring a 'holistic approach' and in being 'open-minded' about both orthodox and complementary medicine, but analysis of the two sets of literature reveals far more similarity than contrast. Nevertheless it was reported by Action for ME that, although the ME charities 'have moved closer together . . . significant differences remain', with little likelihood of a merger. Meanwhile a great deal of energy continues to be expended to vie with one another for the image of being the top ME society.

The American example is a classic illustration of the failure of overlapping associations even to communicate let alone to work together to tackle priority targets. In interview in St Louis the executive director of the American Lung Association's chapter declared that smoking and lung cancer now constituted its 'number one priority'. Coincidentally, and unknown at the time to the interviewer (or, it seems, the executive director), at that very hour elsewhere in St Louis a press conference was being held to announce the launch of 'the biggest ever' anti-smoking campaign in the region. This was a joint initiative of the Medical Society (the doctors' professional body) and the chapter of the American Cancer Society. The Lung Association's top officer, in response to questions about collaborative activity, had few instances to offer and made no mention of this highly topical campaign. She clearly knew nothing about it, and the Cancer Society had not suggested a three-way initiative despite the two organizations having shared medical priorities (and being located in offices less than two miles apart). It is this competitive autonomy which Americans label critically as 'turfism'. A more trivial, but equally significant, instance of it arose in Chapter 3: the executive director of the American Diabetes Association in St Louis did not even know the name of the opposite number at the Juvenile Diabetes Foundation.

What is being suggested here is this: autonomy and diversity are key strengths of patients' associations. Separateness, specialization and (often) smallness ensure a plethora of channels through which energy and enthusiasm can flourish. Turfism may be a necessary price to pay for these benefits, but there is a cost. The political economy of patients' associations includes structural limitations to their collective financial and managerial effectiveness (in Chapter 6 the consequences of turfism for political effectiveness will be added). These limitations could be tackled, at least in part, through agreements to collaborate in the provision of basic organizational infrastructure (offices and equipment), but the chances of this happening seem slight. In Britain the culture of volunteerism militates against such change, while in America turfism is so embedded in associations that even modest attempts to encourage cooperation, such as that of the Combined Health Appeal in St Louis, get little or no response: to have an office of one's own, however tiny, is viewed as symbolizing strength and maturity.

CONCLUSIONS

Vibrant and lively as the world of patients' associations undoubtedly is, it is not without its downside. Its very strengths are also its potential weaknesses. Excessive competition for funds, for support from experts, and for market niche all give rise to activities which need to be scrutinized to ensure their cost-effectiveness. Unfortunately the main external watchdogs, the bodies which license, regulate and audit the financial affairs of patients' associations, are alone inadequate. And internally, associations are in general manned and monitored by supporters who are naturally full of goodwill and trust. Even where the larger associations bring in outsiders to serve as honorary members of boards (more common in America, as is seen in Chapter 8), the culture of philanthropy runs strongly. While this is as it should be, there is a potential cost of limited critical questioning of activities and accounts.

There is no easy solution to this. The NHS experience of appointing five non-executive directors to each health agency as part of the 1989–91 reforms, including payment of a small fee, did not lead to obviously improved local monitoring and indeed was soon accompanied by increased centralization of accountability (Baggott 1998). The more complex American regulation of charities through both federal and state-level agencies has not prevented cases of financial fraud and abuse there. The UK Charity Commission, which was found to have failed badly in the 1980s (National Audit Office 1987), has been strengthened but the sheer number of charities, a doubling to over 154,000 in the period 1968–85 (Ware 1989: 158) and close to 200,000 by the end of the twentieth century with a net increase of at least 3000 new registrations every year from 1977 to 1993 in the detailed data (Kendall and Knapp 1996: table 1.1) ensures that it cannot play a hands-on role. In 1987 it had but 330 staff, implying that each could effectively monitor close to 500 charities: in practice it could only respond to complaints and was unable even to undertake random spot checks (Ware 1989: 208). Until the Charity Commissioners are further strengthened, and one area for debate is whether they should be given legal powers to appoint at least one independent member to each charity's board, the main scrutiny will continue to be the standard process of external auditing of accounts. That process, and each charity chooses its own auditors, inevitably concentrates on narrow financial regularity and probity whereas many of the potential weaknesses in the political economy of associations have here been identified as relating to important but far broader considerations of organization, purpose and activity.

6

THE POLITICAL EFFECTIVENESS OF PATIENT'S ASSOCIATIONS

Whatever they may say, disease-related patients' associations are clearly a political phenomenon. Their routine protestations to the contrary commonly eschew politics. All but a few claim to be non-political support groups. Many are at first sight exactly that and no more, particularly the 50 per cent or so that are run on an all-volunteer or almost all-volunteer basis. However, in Chapter 2 'political' was defined as embracing any activity likely to influence the allocation of resources within society and the provision of health services. As a result, the self-help and support activities of even the most seemingly non-political of associations must be interpreted as political if only because one outcome is the transmission of awareness of good practice, leading to increased expectations and demands from patients and carers. Health care providers are pressurized to modify care and treatment regimes as a consequence.

Political behaviour, in this chapter, thus ranges from low-key and often indirect activity through to overt campaigning to alter laws, entitlements, access to care, and budgets; from micro- to macropolitics. Rarely is it partisan: macropolitics targets all political parties and governments (and their agencies including, for example, bodies licensing drugs and equipment and regulating health professionals), while micropolitics is usually centred on individual providers, notably doctors. In between is the intermediate level: the hospital, local health board or sub-national government agency, collective payer or provider, any of which may be influenced to change administrative (including access to care) or budgetary policies or procedures.

Before examining the record of political activity in detail, three main categories of political resources potentially available to patients' associations are identified. Some automatically accrue to patients' associations; others have to be positively acquired by them. Some are routinely in play on a daily basis as part of the normal interaction between doctors and patients, and between members or officers of associations and health care institutions and providers. Others are only deployed intermittently, through conscious choice. It is important to establish to what extent self-styled 'non-political' bodies are imbued with political resources, and in what ways those resources might (whether consciously or unwittingly) be mobilized. Only at that point can the political performance of associations begin to be evaluated: both their actual effectiveness and their potential effectiveness should they appear to be 'underperforming'. The extent to which patients' associations can offer a real challenge to existing health care systems is a topic to which Chapter 10 returns.

POLITICAL RESOURCES

In Chapter 2 a dozen or so political resources potentially available to patients' associations were identified under three broad headings: tangible, behavioural and image-related.

Tangible resources have been described as 'sanctional' (Allison 1975: 113) in that possession of them allegedly gives a group bargaining power. In the case of patients' associations this label applies only rarely, but it should not be entirely discounted. It does not apply to the key political resource available to the general public in liberal democracies: *votes*. Deploying votes to challenge politicians is not only logistically impossible when members and supporters of associations are geographically scattered, and associations collectively are fragmented, but is also very risky because of likely damage to the image of non-partisanship and philanthropy to which health charities aspire. In addition, legal status as a charity would be threatened by such partisan action. Yet there are health charities which do venture into lobbying activities during election campaigns. In the run up to the British general election of May 1997, for example, an HIV/AIDS group in Manchester, the George House Trust, quizzed candidates by post about their attitudes to a range of issues about AIDS and circulated the responses to its supporters and the media. However, it drew back from explicitly recommending how to vote.

Associations collectively may indeed be 'big business' but

money, another of Allison's sanctional political resources, is equally unlikely to be openly deployed in political campaigning by charities. Yet there clearly is scope for influencing the health research and development agenda when the bigger fund-raisers disburse a large, sometimes a dominant, share of total research spend on a particular medical condition. Involvement in *service delivery and policy implementation* constitutes the third sanctional resource. Several large associations directly provide services funded by donations, while some also have contracts with payers. Although withdrawal from such activity would leave a gap which mainstream providers might find it necessary to fill, possibly not easily or as economically, any serious threat to withdraw services is an unlikely event as no association would want to abandon activities valued by its members. However, service provision and large-scale financial support for research give an association expertise, legitimacy, and ready and regular access to health policy makers.

A key political resource which many associations would dearly like to possess is indeed *access* to payers and providers. Routine access enhances the possibility of influence over a wider range of policy than the particular issue giving rise to that access. 'Insider status' has long been seen by social scientists as significant, giving a group a 'favoured position' (Moran 1989: 123) and activity levels (such as service provision and research funding) which, loosely speaking, make an association a 'partner' in the delivery of health care, constitute a significant move towards this status. Other conscious attempts to enhance access also occur. They range from the recruitment by associations of policy makers as honorary members, to the circulation of literature to, and the organization of seminars and conferences for health professionals.

Associations, then, have some but not many tangible political resources. Most of them particularly lack two available to interest groups in other policy areas, *control over jobs and the information of others* (Polsby 1963: 119–20). There are exceptions, almost always amongst the few sizeable patients' associations. Those providing care services, charitably or under contract with health care payer bodies, employ health professionals. Three British associations with NHS contracts referred to pressures on them from the new (1990s) competitive climate following the introduction of the quasi-market. Others participate in professional training required for accreditation and in continuing professional education. Then there are a few, particularly in Britain in the area of mental illness, with expertise which has led them to be co-opted on to government policy review taskforces. Very occasionally an association is even more integrated on an ongoing basis into policy making than that: the (UK) National Asthma Campaign, for example, administers the NHS research and development programme on asthma management, with responsibility for allocating a budget of £5 million over the five years of the current programme. These, however, are the exceptions: in general, although policy makers may be grateful from time to time for data collated by health charities, both the British and American health care systems exhibit low levels of dependence on these associational activities.

Behavioural political resources, the second type, embrace styles of leadership and lobbying strategies and tactics in the search for access to the policy making arena. The list of such resources includes *social status*. In Chapter 3 it was noted that many associations consciously seek to cultivate social acceptance, and hence political legitimacy, through the recruitment of well known people. So, too, do associations seek to establish their credentials as *expert* bodies with a consequent legitimate stake in health policy formulation. To expertise should be added *representation*: the now widely accepted 'right' of minorities, consumers and service users to a voice, with that voice exercised on their behalf by a specialized association with expert knowledge of their needs (and demands). The host of strategic and tactical decisions confronting associations include how to *interface* with health care payers, providers and policy makers; how to *market* products like newsletters and conferences; and how to relate to the *media*, including the health trade press (proactively or reactively, for example).

For many patients' associations, especially the small and medium-sized ones which make up the vast majority, the most telling behavioural political resources are far more simple than most of those above – yet are potentially at least as effective. *Time, energy* and *focus* are all significant. Whilst senior health policy makers face crowded diaries and juggle with a variety of issues and crises, specialist patients' associations can concentrate on a single issue. The trap they must avoid is that to be effective these resources must be deployed sensitively and sparingly to avoid creating a counter-productive boredom threshold amongst those targeted.

The third type of political resource potentially available to associations centres on their *image*. From image stems 'legitimacy', and legitimacy enhances the prospects of exerting influence. Here a contradiction is immediately apparent between the *beliefs* of the general public and those of policy makers. Associations in the personal health field strike a favourable chord publicly, with an image of philanthropy, charity, volunteerism and 'good works' naturally attached to them. This enables them collectively (they may compete with one another individually) to amass support and funds. Any public petitions they sponsor (the surveys found this to be in both countries a fairly rare activity) will be signed and their collecting boxes filled because of this belief in their legitimacy.

Policy makers, on the other hand, tend to view associations very differently, and much more sceptically. The image now is no longer necessarily positive. Policy makers label specialized associations as sectional groups, pursuing only their narrow self-interests in the specifics of a particular disease and its treatment. A 1994–6 study of British user groups in the fields of mental health and physical disability found health managers to be 'ostensibly overwhelmingly in favour of user involvement in general' but this 'was tempered by . . . criticisms of the groups' including doubts about their management skills as well as about their representativeness and legitimacy (Harrison and Mort 1998: 65–6). They were seen by doctors and managers interviewed as 'neither representative of society at large, nor of all users', and their concerns were influential only when it suited management in internal policy debates, a tactic styled 'playing the user card' (Harrison *et al.* 1997: 10–13). Often their agendas conflicted with the wider public and patient interest which the respondent managers and doctors claimed themselves to represent.

In both countries many wider instances of such conflict arose from the survey material. These include demands from associations for greater spending on particular new treatment regimes as pharmaceutical companies develop new products to either combat or relieve chronic diseases, demands countered by policy makers' concerns about costs and budgets, including problems of locating additional cash (if none is available, the argument moves on to 'one disease's expansion is another's cut' should budgetary redeployment be required). Although this debate has been sharper in Britain's NHS (over beta-interferon, not widely available to people with multiple sclerosis for example), it is not dissimilar in America, particularly within the Medicare and Medicaid systems. Patients' associations are not automatically seen as the legitimate voice of the patient or as representing public opinion in general, and they have to work at achieving access to policy makers through deploying their other political resources.

To sum up: associations do have a range of political resources – tangible, behavioural and image-related – available to them. The potential is there to exercise some political influence over health policy and provision, but mostly this is no more than potential and, because beliefs are so central to policy makers' behaviour, associations have to work hard to mobilize their resources and exert influence at the collective levels of health policy making.

INFLUENCING INDIVIDUAL PROFESSIONALS: THE MICRO LEVEL

Indirect influence at the micro level dominates the political activity of the majority of disease-related patients' associations in both Britain and America. This operates through a combination of patient education and public awareness policies. Virtually every association has a regular newsletter, ostensibly to keep members in touch with the association but also to convey information and thus enhance that political resource of individual members and supporters. In addition to the newsletter, pamphlets, leaflets and other literature are used to make patients and carers aware of the experiences of others with a particular medical condition; aware of new treatment techniques and drug regimes; and aware of the different facilities and approaches adopted in different places. In short, associations sing the praises of exemplars of 'good practice'. When patients interact with doctors and other health professionals there are raised expectations of, and demands for, top quality health care services.

This communication between associations and members is valued in itself by those with a particular condition. It offers a form of support: one is not alone in experiencing that condition, and there may well be some comfort in knowing how the disease might develop and in getting tips from fellow patients. But it is also potentially a political activity. It changes the nature of the individual doctor/patient relationship, and cumulatively it can alter provider and payer attitudes towards a condition as increasing numbers of professionals are faced with requests for reported 'best practice' treatments. In Britain the push by the Multiple Sclerosis Society in the late 1990s to get beta-interferon prescribed more widely included a patient information strategy which helped to pressurize NHS policy makers to develop clinical protocols as advice to doctors. A decade earlier, American AIDS groups had encouraged individual patient protest as part of their campaign to get the then new drug AZT licensed.

All but the most amateur of newsletters are nowadays nicely produced and printed, glossy and in more than two colours, thanks to affordable desktop publishing technology. Surprisingly, the overall standard of newsletters from the small all-volunteer British associations compared very favourably with their American national equivalents, and with many of the productions of the office-based chapters in St Louis. Most, in both countries, appear quarterly, commonly carrying members' actual experiences of care and treatment, expert answers to queries (by doctors and other health professionals), accounts of fund-raising activities and social events, and news of the latest research findings and of possible 'breakthroughs' in the battle against disease. The overall objective is to raise morale and encourage more support. As noted in Chapter 3, associations have consciously developed corporate images with logos and mottoes prominent and snappy newsletter titles. The most recent development in 1997–8 was the increased creation of Web pages as a new source of publicity and member information.

The Craniofacial Support Group, for example, was founded in Britain only in 1993 and by 1997 had a mailing list of no more than 500. By then its (three editions a year) *Headlines* ran to 32 pages. The National Back Pain Association's glossy quarterly *Talkback* of 28 pages had an extra 8 as a supplement for professionals, undoubtedly also examined and digested by the 'amateur' patients. Where there is scope for advertisements from drug or equipment manufacturers, or from food companies where diet is the key treatment (as in the Coeliac Society with its *The Crossed Grain*), newsletters can reach up to 72 or more pages, and bring in considerable income. In addition, many associations publish annual or biannual magazines aimed at a mixture of professionals and patients. The apparent political incorrectness of several British titles is presumably only acceptable to some association members because the association's themselves invented the titles. Take for example *Quiet* (British Tinnitus Association); *Spin* (Ménière's Society); *Side View* (Macular Disease Society – damaged eye membrane); *Step Forward* (Limbless Association); and *Chew* (Tracheo Oesophageal Fistula Support Group – babies born unable to swallow).

The conscious attempt to 'educate' health professionals is another political activity targeting the micro level of individual provider behaviour. The larger and more established American and British associations have stated objectives which include professional education. The Eating Disorders Association in Britain was one to introduce a new category of 'professional member' in the 1990s and it now publishes a quarterly professional journal, *European Eating Disorders Review*, and periodically runs training courses. In 1996 the National Eczema Society ran 23 courses for nurses, 3 for doctors and 6 for pharmacists. Some 400 health professionals attended five regional conferences across Britain organized in 1996–7 by the National Asthma Campaign, noted earlier as also managing the NHS budget for asthma management research.

Many American associations also regularly interface with health professionals. Some host very prestigious national (and international) conferences, often incurring considerable costs through speakers' fees and participants' hospitality (top American doctors and health professionals expect rather more pampering than is traditionally offered in Britain). The Arizona-based Muscular Dystrophy Association is a typical instance. As well as offering traditional workshops it now uses the internet to provide electronic seminars and conferences, spending almost 20 per cent of its US$77 million expenditure on programmes and services in 1996–7 on 'professional and public health education' (US$15 million).

In addition to conference and seminar activity, the National Osteoporosis Foundation (NOF) typifies many others in America in publishing a quarterly bulletin ('Clinical Updates') aimed solely at doctors – in this case at primary care physicians. It also has a category of professional membership, and in late 1997 NOF planned to publish its own clinical practice guidelines. Its June 1997 Fourth International Symposium, co-sponsored by four of the specialist National Institutes of Health, attracted a worldwide attendance of more than 1600 doctors, scientists and health professionals. Founded only in 1986, NOF has quickly become recognized as a legitimate and a significant partner by mainstream policy making and professional bodies, yet a staff of only 17 and a budget of only US$1.6 million in 1996 by no means make it giant-sized.

The engine room of the interface between the patients' association and the individual health professional in America, however, might be expected to be found at the local chapter level, explored in detail in Chapter 8. Good geographical reasons for this include not just travel logistics but also the existence for each health professional of different licensing rules and Medicaid provider regulations and policies in each state. This gives scope for a variety of tailor-made programmes in medicine, nursing and therapy and in health systems and procedures, offering chapters an obvious niche. Activity varies, with some chapters doing little more than provide a top national expert speaker at a single annual dinner for doctors (often sponsored by drug companies). Other chapters are much more proactive. The (medium-sized) Leukemia Society of America offers an annual professional conference and, separately, a specialised workshop. The Epilepsy Foundation reported 790 participants at its 19 professional education seminars held in St Louis in 1996. The US$100,000 spent annually on professional education by the Multiple Sclerosis Society chapter included courses for a range of providers from doctors to aquatic instructors.

In St Louis most of the thirty or so office-based chapters reported regular contact with professional providers of treatment and care, and doctors are almost always found among the board members. Separate medical advisory panels are also commonplace, even where the chapter has no research funds to allocate (in some cases, including the Juvenile Diabetes Foundation, all revenues raised go to national headquarters for allocation to selected projects). However, documentation indicates that several interviewee claims of professional contact were not sustainable because they were tokenistic: the single sponsored annual dinner, sometimes with not even a medical or other expert speaker. Chapter 8 concludes that at the association/professional interface, many St Louis chapters underperformed politically: any micro level political influence was dependent more on the demands of individual patients.

INFLUENCING INSTITUTIONS: THE INTERMEDIATE LEVEL

Patients' associations have a range of concerns at the intermediate level between individual providers and national policy: the hospital, provider or payer organization, insurer, health board or state government. These concerns include access to care and often centre on issues relating to the availability of specialist treatment skills and facilities, the provision of state-of-the-art diagnostic equipment and the use of the latest treatment regimes.

The environment within which associations operate is slightly different in the two countries. Although in both the access issue is in essence about responsibility for meeting the costs of health care, in Britain access itself is the central concern of many patients' associations because NHS authorities have historically been slow to invest in new technology and treatments. The regional offices of the Department of Health, the local health authorities (which commission and pay for NHS services), and NHS Trusts (which provide those services) are the key organizations at the intermediate level.

In America, the extent to which patients are expected themselves to pay for care (and provision is often expensive as in the cases of scanners or new drugs) is a major factor driving many patients' associations into political action. Their main targets at the intermediate level include hospitals (often now part of a chain), the burgeoning numbers of managed care organizations, and state legislatures and agencies which determine the scope and scale of the Medicaid programme, administer Medicare and Medicaid, monitor service quality through PROs (peer review organizations), and license hospitals and health professionals.

The chapters in St Louis found the fragmentation of health care provision a major obstacle. They commonly sought to include representation from hospitals and managed care organizations, in particular, on their management boards, and some expressed satisfaction at this link. Representation, however, in no way means that the individuals concerned attempt to act as 'representatives'. The key to understanding American health care is to think of it as based on capitalist behaviour. There is fierce competition between hospitals for patients, with massive overbedding, low occupancy rates, and literally thousands of mothballed beds. Just as fierce is the competition between managed care organizations and other insurers for patients. In this climate it is 'every man for himself' and the inclusion of a manager from one hospital on an association's board in no way indicates that an exchange of ideas across the hospital sector takes place. That manager may have a strong empathy with the cause which an association represents, but he or she is also always conscious of the creation of new market opportunities.

Associations seem not to attempt to influence providers at collective settings. Most American patients' associations are well used to manning stalls at health fairs and similar events aimed at the general public, with the usual display equipment. Beyond that there lay a big gap. Attendance, twice, at the annual three-day Missouri Hospitals Association Convention, a very large gathering of a thousand delegates, revealed that in neither year did the 130 exhibitors include a single patients' association, nor did any association provide a speaker at the scores of fringe meetings. (The 'turfism' uncovered in Chapter 5 precluded the possibility of a joint exhibit or presentation). Interviews at the Missouri Patient Care Review Foundation (the state PRO) also revealed no evidence of an interface (occasional or regular) with patients' associations, despite its proactive pursuit of projects to raise the quality of care:

in 1997 these included diabetes management, stroke prevention and congestive heart failure treatment, all issues clearly central to the mission of local chapters.

Hospitals individually in St Louis claimed to be active both in hosting support groups and in listening to patients' voices. They do indeed pursue both lines of activity, but for the most part they act autonomously rather than by working alongside patients' associations. Only a small number of associations meet or operate in hospital facilities (mainly the all-volunteer ones, with no office space) and one established association – Parkinson Disease Association – is based in a specialist teaching hospital, but the study of a typical large suburban general hospital revealed that it conducts its own patient satisfaction surveys, operates its own support groups in areas like stroke rehabilitation and breast cancer, and publishes its own leaflets on a wide variety of conditions rather than using those produced by patients' associations. The hospital was offering 25 Health and Wellness programmes, with only the American Red Cross as a partner (for first aid training).

The emerging picture in America, then, is of a combination of inaction by, and of the widespread exclusion of patients' associations at the hospital level. There remains the possibility of political activity centred around the state legislature and government.

The Alzheimer's Association (AA) was one of few associations openly pursuing a political role. In 1995 it appointed (jointly with other Missouri chapters of AA, and pump-primed by the national office) a public policy coordinator with a US$50,000 budget (5 per cent of its total spend). In 1996–7 a four-pronged strategy was approved by the board. The state legislators were to be pressed to provide some US$250,000 of public monies for research into the disease and a similar sum for grants to establish new services – amounts deliberately pitched at fairly modest levels to attract support for a 'reasonable' request, though this lobbying followed failure to get the two schemes into the state budget owing to a veto by the governor who was opposed to any increased public spending. Other campaigns were for legislation to prevent 'impaired drivers' (people with Alzheimer's disease and similar conditions) from driving by tightening up licence conditions; and for protected entitlements to long-term care services for Medicaid patients. A database of about 1100 volunteers had been built up by the coordinator and each was asked to write to selected senators and House representatives calling for the relevant legislative committees to hold public hearings. In Missouri written and oral evidence is given at such hearings and is then published. Some preliminary private hearings were in progress at the time of the interviews.

As in Britain, the American associations in the mental illness field are also politically overtly active. Here the focus again is on evidence from the St Louis case study, analysed at length in Chapter 8. The Alliance for the Mentally Ill, when interviewed in November 1997, had been active in three policy areas.

First, the Alliance had successfully pressed the state legislature for clarification of the law on the compulsory hospitalization of psychiatric patients following the tragic murder by a schizophrenic of his parents. There are clear parallels here with recent British debates, also in the wake of tragic events, about whether the mentally ill in the community should be compulsorily removed to hospital if they do not comply voluntarily with prescribed treatment. A bill was drafted and passed in Missouri, though its implementation looked to be patchy.

A second 1997 campaign had sought parity of health care entitlements with the physically ill: some insurers offered a lifetime ceiling of US$1 million for the latter but as little as US$50,000 for psychiatric patients. By the end of 1997 the state legislature had approved compulsory parity in the case of managed care organizations but not from insurers operating on the traditional fee-for-service basis.

Finally, the privatization of directly provided state Medicaid services for the poor remained a concern, with attempts to ensure that costs were not cut by contracts failing to specify adequate service levels. A Bill was being drafted by the Alliance to prevent the Medicaid contractors (managed care organizations) from providing no more than a medical diagnosis, without proper back-up counselling, therapy or other community services.

In stark contrast to this level of ongoing political activity, many other chapters replied in similar vein to the executive director of the Crohn's and Colitis Foundation who, when asked about lobbying, replied 'we are not into this at all'. The Asthma and Allergy Foundation concurred, but later claimed to be trying to pressurize insurers to recognize and pay for certain unorthodox 'drugs' such as herbal remedies. However, its literature was completely bereft of signs of concerted action, and this looked like a 'wish list' item. The National Neurofibromatosis Foundation wanted the state licensing board for doctors to include a question about the disease on its examination paper, but, similarly, there was no strategy for achieving it, the only political goal raised. The Amyotrophic Lateral Sclerosis

Association (ALSA) (motor neurone disease) responded: 'we have minimal relations with health officials, except on behalf of an individual patient'. Such advocacy work is potentially politically significant as the successful redress of grievance can modify subsequent provision and policy, though ALSA had not thought of it in those terms.

British experience is not dissimilar. Evidence of concerted lobbying of local health authorities and NHS Trusts by disease-related patients' associations tends to be limited to issues surrounding HIV/AIDS and mental illness (if disability is excluded as those associations mostly did not meet the criteria for inclusion in this study). Thus 'influencing decision-makers' is the first stated aim of the National Schizophrenia Fellowship, and it has actively campaigned in many localities (as well as nationally) for more community psychiatric nurses. Intermediate-level campaigning tends to arise when access to care is perceived as a problem, though this is often presented publicly as a concern about quality. Although NHS principles embrace equity of access based only on clinical need, in practice, service levels and quality standards vary considerably from place to place, particularly in the cases of high cost or highly specialized areas of medicine.

The Primary Immunodeficiency Association, for example, decided to mount a lobbying campaign aimed at selected health authorities after a 'systematic comparison of treatment available'. The Spinal Injuries Association persuaded the NHS (Northern Region) to replace its specialist centre with a new one. A separate campaign included the circulation of treatment recommendations ('A Charter for Support') to every NHS Trust. The National Osteoporosis Society surveyed health authorities in 1996, publishing a report that more than half of them had failed to implement 1995 government recommendations on the management of osteoporosis, while in 1997 Alzheimer's Disease Society was critical of low spending by several named health authorities. Gaucher's Association (an inherited enzyme deficiency disorder) and the British Stammering Association both sought to 'encourage' better availability of treatment. How the former, a tiny all-volunteer body in an area of medicine with only 226 known sufferers, planned to achieve this was unclear, and the latter's listed aims and objectives were very non-political.

As in America, the British survey revealed plenty of wish lists and some spasmodic one-off political activity targeting the intermediate level, but hard evidence of overt and sustained political action which is effective in influencing health care provision at this level was scarce. The examples above were noticeably all of British national associations choosing to focus on local issues, and not of local branches, in sharp contrast to the American evidence of chapter-level activity. This contrasting local political behaviour is a central feature of the detailed case study of St Louis and Greater Manchester presented in Chapters 8 and 9.

MACROPOLITICS: POLITICAL CAMPAIGNING AT THE NATIONAL LEVEL

At the national level, political action can be expected to target government – in Britain because it is responsible for the NHS, and in America because private sector payers and providers do not operate nationwide (exceptionally a few hospital chains do operate in many states), but the federal government's Medicare programme for the elderly and disabled is universal and it also lays down the framework of the Medicaid programme for the poor, administered variably from state to state through a system of exemptions known as federal waivers. In addition, in both countries there is a perceived national responsibility for public health issues ranging from patient-centred prevention (such as vaccinations) through the regulation and approval of drugs to more general matters such as 'mad cow disease' in Britain, services for the American Indians and for armed forces veterans in America, and research and development programmes in both.

American HIV/AIDS associations flexed their political muscles in the early 1990s at the federal level over the licensing of the hoped-for new 'wonder drug' AZT. The federal regulatory agency and the executive and legislative branches of government were all lobbied to speed up approval for general use and for large-scale experimental licensing. In this case political pressure was exercised very overtly, using just about every type of public campaign. Slightly less noisily the American Lung Association continues to press publicly for the greater regulation of tobacco sales to young people. It even took out a 'friendly lawsuit' against the EPA (Environmental Protection Agency), seeking an order to force it to review and tighten its air quality standards because of concerns about asthma (friendly because EPA wanted judicial confirmation of its ability to revisit existing standards).

However, most of the political activity of American patients' associations is exercised rather more quietly. Typically, national offices use local chapters to synchronize the lobbying of federal politicians alongside their attempts at gaining access to politicians and bureaucrats in Washington. Often, chapter action includes write-in campaigns by local members and supporters. Some press coverage is sought, though usually not of a sensational nature because the objective is to alert politicians to the 'problem' by 'briefing' them, and not to alienate them.

Concern with the alleged slowness of new drugs receiving approval (because the regulators seek robust evidence about impact and side-effects from randomized controlled trials over several years) has led others in America to lobby too: the National Multiple Sclerosis Society (NMSS) over beta-interferon, for instance. NMSS is also one of several to regularly remind federal politicians of the case for greater public funding of the National Institutes for Health, the central agencies in medical research and development, and through this the greater funding of 'their' specialized field of interest. The Lupus Foundation of America initiated a Congressional bill to increase research funding but, like many such bills, it fell victim to the complex legislative process and made no real progress. In contrast, the American Diabetes Association claimed in interview that its lobbying, based on league table data showing underfunding compared to other conditions, led directly to President Clinton allocating an extra US$30 million to diabetes research in 1996–7. In all these examples the symbiotic relationship between associations and the medical research community, first noted in the discussion of potential professional colonization in Chapter 5, is apparent.

The centralized British welfare state widens the range of issues on which associations might lobby at the national level. Drug approval and research funding are common concerns in Britain too, but campaigning goes well beyond this. For example Action for ME (and chronic fatigue) claims that its lobbying persuaded the NHS Pensions Agency to grant pensions to NHS staff retiring due to the onset of ME – a condition not previously recognised as an illness. This is disputed by the competing ME Association, which dates its campaigning on recognition back to a 1987 Department of Health decision. The Association for Spina Bifida and Hydrocephalus (annual report: 'we continue to be an influence on government') helped to persuade the Department of Health in 1992 to promulgate official government advice to pregnant women to take folic acid to reduce the chances of abnormal births.

In these instances 'campaigning' is, as in America, typically quiet and semi-private. It may involve Members of Parliament, but executive power in Britain is so marked that civil servants and ministers are the real targets. Within Parliament several all-party groups (often of both MPs and Lords) with specialized interests provide the setting for low-key publicity, and facilitate access to the real policy makers. Thus Headway National Head Injuries Association uses an all-party group of politicians to highlight its call for head injuries to be recognized as a 'separate disability' for social security entitlements. And the National Osteoporosis Society helped launch a new all-party group in 1996, immediately using it to lobby government (unsuccessfully) to include targets for tackling osteoporosis in its 'Health of the Nation' public health policy.

'Campaigning' is a term used very variably by British associations. The examples above all fall near the middle of a continuum ranging from working with government in campaigns targeting the public, to open political pressure attacking government policy. At one end lie associations such as the Foundation for the Study of Infant Deaths, with its 1996 'Reduce the Risk Campaign', run 'in partnership with the Department of Health'. The campaign itself might be classified as non-political, but it stemmed from political lobbying to create the partnership.

At the other end of this continuum are open campaigns to change government policy. The Stroke Association delivered a 10,000-name petition to the Prime Minister in October 1997, with 300 supporters simultaneously lobbying their MPs, demanding specialist stroke units in hospitals and specialized home carers to support those discharged from hospital. This campaign continues and is a fairly unusual British instance of sustained efforts to achieve media coverage as a political resource. (Unusual for two reasons: few campaigns are sustained over many months at such a high level of activity as this one; and publicity is usually viewed as a not very effective political tool – if specialist services do result on any large scale, analysts of pressure groups will need to revisit conventional thinking). The Haemophilia Society also opted for tactics of sustained pressure using publicity. Since 1995 it has sought financial aid for those infected (via blood products) with Hepatitis C on similar terms to those infected with HIV. The Major government refused and in 1996 a 30,000-name petition went to the Prime Minister, a mass lobby of Parliament took place and over 270 MPs signed a critical motion.

In both countries the centre of the continuum is occupied far more than are the ends. Health politics is largely played out in a dignified way, not exactly in private but away from the mass media. The health trade press might well be involved, but not the tabloids or television. Exceptions arise, especially when life-threatening conditions are linked to ethical and moral considerations (in America the AZT issue was one instance of mass media interest). But most associations demand nothing as sensational (in news terms) as this: indeed, many could be accused of being almost too reasonable or undemanding, publicly at any rate.

In Britain the Motor Neurone Disease Association reported in 1997 that the new drug Riluzole seemed very promising but that the 'hard realities of NHS budgets' meant that many would not get it. Simultaneously the Alzheimer's Disease Society complained in its members' newsletter that another new drug, Aricept, was being 'blocked by ministers' for cost reasons. In neither case was a campaign of public pressure launched because health politics are played out in a non-partisan environment which, in Britain, sees associations accepting the financial necessity for limitations on access to care, or in other words accepting some level of rationing.

Associations are cautious about publicly challenging this bi-partisan NHS political culture of cost containment. They fear that any apparent refusal to keep within the unwritten rules of the game might have wider consequences such as a lack of access to policy makers. The negative side of their public image could be brought into play, and they want to avoid being portrayed as narrow and self-interested bodies with no political legitimacy. During one interview in St Louis, attempts to explain to officials of the American Multiple Sclerosis Society the limited NHS use of beta-interferon highlighted the different parameters within which British and American associations operate: rationing is not an acceptable explanation for public policy in America.

Parameters within which associations feel obliged to operate also exist in America, though they are different, reflecting its politics of health. The 1992–4 Clinton reform plan, hotly and widely debated but not enacted, provides an interesting example. Because debate was partisan, and because American patients' associations both consciously cultivate a non-partisan image and practically seek tangible support from all sectors of society, few were prepared to take a firm stance on the package as a whole. The Alzheimer's Association (AA) chapter officials in St Louis put it like this: the national association had its own bus touring America alongside the federal government's 'caravan' as part of the programme of public meetings chaired by Mrs Clinton but instructions were clear: 'AA is not endorsing the plan but is endorsing long-term care entitlements'. Selective support for parts of the Clinton plan was a tactic others adopted, including the American Association for Retired Persons (Skocpol 1996: ch. 3). Similarly, within Missouri, AA chose not to give public testimony in 1996–7 on a bill to regulate managed care because the draft bill was 'too big and wide-ranging'. Its width made the bill extremely controversial and tricky to handle: the AA chapter board, for example, included health insurers with direct interests in the contents so it was politic to avoid debate by an officer-level decision to restrict political activity to narrower but important issues.

At all three levels – micro, intermediate and macro – patient association politics has been analysed so far in this chapter on the basis of the individual association. Given that many health issues (of cost, of quality and of access) are common to several associations, either because they represent a particular medical condition or because the underlying issue is one of principle affecting a range of conditions (as with the introduction of new 'wonder' drugs), there seems to be a great deal of scope for alliances, coalitions or concerted action across associations. It is, after all, a common belief that 'unity is strength' in the exercise of power and influence. The final section of this chapter examines the evidence of collaborative political activity, concluding that in both Britain and America the potential remains largely unfulfilled.

COLLABORATIVE POLITICS

With just a handful of exceptions, the overall picture is one of the failure of disease-related patients' associations to work together to increase their ability to influence policy makers. The turfism uncovered in Chapter 5 severely inhibits their political role in both countries. The combination of effective political resources such as expertise, contacts, access routes and public sympathy is rarely fully exploited through alliances, coalitions or other interactive approaches.

The emphasis in this section is on continuing collaboration. Sporadic joint action, usually around a single event (the British associations working in the area of breast cancer care have occasionally collaborated in public demonstrations, for example) does occur but is not studied here. A new style of joint action, linking associations with health institutions is also emerging. Jointly sponsored conferences and seminars for professionals are one indicator; joint surveys and research studies are another. A major instance of the latter is given below, in the discussion of the Long-term Medical Conditions Alliance, an established British organization. Another British example linked the Stroke Association with two other consumer bodies and the Royal College of Physicians. A joint 1998 survey revealed alarming numbers of diagnostic and treatment errors (Royal College of Physicians 1999) and the Association hoped that the College's imprimatur would ensure that forthcoming national clinical guidelines enhanced the quality of services.

Though American officials spoke loosely of coalitions and joint working, analysis of interviews in St Louis and of associations' national literature indicates a dearth of examples of sustained political activity across associations on medical issues (examples of coalitions on welfare and disability issues were far more frequently cited in interviews). Indeed, there is much evidence to the contrary. In Chapter 5 the total failure of the cancer and lung associations to work together on the 1997 Missouri anti-smoking campaign emerged. The complete failure of five competing Parkinson's disease charities to work together nationally led an Arizona congressman to table a bill in frustration. The Udal Bill, which did not progress, sought a US$100 million National Institutes of Health allocation for research. Although two of the five associations, based in Chicago and New York, almost merged, after talks they remained as separate competitors. Potential initiators of political alliances might be the two American cooperative fund-raisers, United Way and the Combined Health Appeal. However, because they are highly unlikely to instigate effective collaboration their work is discussed more fully in Chapter 8 rather than here.

In contrast to American fragmentation, the British survey material revealed several attempts to establish genuinely collaborative political lobbying on a permanent basis. In particular in four fields (genetics, neurology, chronic illnesses, skin care) ambitious national-level alliances have been attempted. Success has been variable because individual associations value their autonomy and are therefore reluctant to see it reduced unless there are very clear and immediate advantages in prospect. Indeed, differences of both opinion and policy priorities have led to internal divisions and resignations in the cases of two of the four main groupings listed above.

The two most successful have been the Genetic Interest Group (GIG) and the Long-term Medical Conditions Alliance (LMCA), both founded in 1989. GIG had over one hundred charities in membership and a paid staff of six by 1997. Its primary goal is 'to promote awareness and understanding of genetic disorders in order that high quality services ... may be developed or sustained'. Membership includes both local and national charities, but also some hospital departments so it is more than just a patient-led group. The Neurological Alliance is smaller but growing, and the Skin Care Campaign is the smallest of these four coalitions.

The focus here is on the third grouping, the Long-term Medical Conditions Alliance. LMCA is of particular interest for two reasons. First it is composed solely of patient-led associations and second because it is beginning to experience political success in terms of obtaining legitimacy in the eyes of NHS policy makers and consequently of access and 'insider status'. Yet it only employed its first paid officer in late 1996, and when studied in early 1998 it remained tiny with just two staff (later, in November 1998, it was to receive a National Lottery award of £170,000 over three years to underpin its 'development work with member organizations, one-third of whom rely on volunteers and trustees to keep running'). Its founders were in four separate, small alliances in the 1980s. They formed LMCA in 1989 for similar reasons to those which led to GIG being founded: serious shared concerns about the possible negative impact of the 1989–91 NHS reforms, with its purchaser/provider split, on people with chronic medical conditions. By early 1998 LMCA had 72 member associations, an increase of eight in the year, and its political legitimacy was underlined when the Junior Minister of Health addressed its annual meeting with a speech that was press-released to the media.

LMCA's success reflects both its policy and its personnel. Its first and only director is an acknowledged expert on self-help groups, having worked to develop their role for many years (*How to Work with Self-help Groups* (Wilson 1995) is her key study of the inter-face between such groups and health professionals). Her approach has been to focus on the case for 'patients' voices' to be heard within the NHS, a subject which both unites associations and reflects the 1990s policy of successive governments. The strategy has been to demonstrate that patients' associations are very good patients' voices, more so than either the general public (most of whom are, happily, in good health and are lacking in personal experience of receiving long-term care) or community health councils (established to represent the general public as part of the 1974 NHS reforms, with some users as members but dominated by political appointees of local authorities).

When Wilson arrived at LMCA in 1996 to transform it from an all-volunteer office she inherited what turned out to be a break-through in developing an interface between the NHS and patients' associations. An action research project across six health authorities involved 14 LMCA members working in twos and threes with a health authority 'to commission quality health services which meet the needs of the patients using them'. The report *Patients Influencing Purchasers* was published in 1997. It contained 16 recommendations along with 26 'lessons' and 22 examples of detailed outcomes in the six areas. Significantly, in terms of political legitimacy, publication was not by LMCA but by the NHS Confederation, the national grouping of health authorities, with an introduction from a junior minister commending the findings (Lewthwaite and Haffenden 1997). Both practically and politically this is in effect a benchmarking report, providing LMCA with an ongoing agenda and the status and image enabling it to step up its campaigning role. It soon began to flex its new muscles. In April 1998 it published demands for earlier referral to specialists to speed up diagnoses, claiming that this 'would have the greatest impact on the quality of life for people with chronic conditions'. Enhanced press coverage of this reflected its growing political legitimacy.

There are three possible explanations of the striking contrast between political alliances in Britain and America. First, American political culture centres on competition, pluralism and fragmentation across both the public and the private sector. Coalitions, necessary to take policy change forward, are temporary and forged on an issue-by-issue basis. Autonomy is the greater prize, and turfism results. Second, American patients associations are faced with multiple targets because there is no health care 'system'. Any alliances might vary from target to target, as well as from issue to issue, and this disjointed environment throws up almost impossible challenges to collaboration, even if there is a will to work together (which there often is not). Furthermore, many of the targets are in the private sector, where actions are less than transparent. In contrast the British associations have both a single target – the NHS – and one which is part of the public sector, with the consequence that public accountability is required of its policy makers. Third, there is a fairly well established tradition of voluntary organizations working on a collaborative basis in Britain. Umbrella bodies like the National Council of Voluntary Organizations exist in every major town and, in the case of the NHS, there has now been a quarter of a century of experience of community health councils.

CONCLUSIONS

The scale and nature of patients' association political activity and influence contrasts sharply both between and within the two countries. There are obvious gaps and differences: little collaboration in America; surprisingly little intermediate-level activity in Britain. On the other hand, targeting the micro level of the individual health professional through individual political action is a comparable political activity, and is more prominent than open campaigning.

The health charities in this study, though claiming to be non-political, actually possess potentially significant political resources, including knowledge and expertise about the diseases which they represent, money for distribution to health researchers, and often great energy and commitment. That they do not always choose to deploy these to influence health care and health policy partly reflects conscious decisions to remain 'non-political' social and support groups but is also partly explained by two significant features which emerged in this chapter: the politically hazardous complex double-image which associations enjoy (philanthropic to some; narrowly self-interested to others); and the fragmentation of authority and health institutions which they perceive. To these may be added a third: a lack of political expertise. Often reference was made above to wish lists and to the apparent absence of clear strategies or tactics for translating patients' associations' demands into public policy. It appears that most charity managers lack basic skills in policy analysis and consequently are unsure how best to take issues forward. Given their backgrounds and ethos, this is perhaps not surprising.

Though most obvious in the pluralistic American 'non-system' of health care provision and policy, institutional and health policy making fragmentation is also evident in Britain. Professional clinical freedom and intermediate-level separate health authority and NHS Trust agencies, each with some power and influence over health care provision, operate within the 'national' concept of the NHS to ensure that services vary up and down the country, not least in the case of specialized care for the minority conditions – the very focus of the patients' associations studied here. With the quasi-market reforms of the 1990s making increasing geographical inequities more explicit (Powell 1998: 66), there is fertile ground on which patients' associations might act to exert influence, though mostly they choose not to do so.

In neither country are patients' associations offering a strong political challenge to established interests. Their influence is at best marginal overall, and significant in only a handful of instances. Their very existence has a quiet impact at the level of the individual patient/professional interface, and their investment in medical research can lead to new treatment and care regimes. This type of activity and influence is not the usual focus of studies of pressure group politics. It is the politics of presence rather than of pressure. Slow changes to values and expectations may lack the excitement of public campaigns, but they most certainly indicate influence. Whether or not disease-related patients' associations have the potential or the ability to mount a serious challenge to existing health care policies and established health interests is a question to which the final chapter will return.

PART III

COMPARING
CONURBATIONS

7

THE ORGANIZATIONAL CONTEXT

The next three chapters provide a comparative case study of patient association activity in two large conurbations: Greater Manchester, England, and Metropolitan St Louis, Missouri, USA. For ease of reading, the shorthand titles of 'Manchester' and 'St Louis' are used.

TWO CONURBATIONS: THE BASIS OF COMPARISON

There are several striking demographic and socio-economic similarities between Manchester and St Louis. Each has a population of between 2.5 and 3.0 million. In both cases the conurbation core, the central city with separate municipal status, experienced rapid population decline from around 700,000 to 400,000 in the second half of the twentieth century, and that decline has seen these centres increasingly populated by the poor and black communities. Suburban growth of middle-class estates has happened on the conurbation fringes, and in both there is a circular motorway/freeway surrounding the area but with residential neighbourhoods stretching for a few miles on both sides of it. Central city economic decline, particularly in the manufacturing sector, has been offset by outer area and service industry growth, most noticeable in the guise of suburban shopping malls and city centre tourist and conference facilities. Though the swathes of unused former industrial and substandard housing areas are more noticeable in St Louis, both conurbations include many 'brownfield' sites.

In other respects, however, there are dissimilarities and even sharp contrasts. Population density is much lower in St Louis, which extends outwards for over twenty-five miles from the centre, twice the radius of Manchester. The latter has a ring of old industrial towns at the core of its suburbs – Bolton, Oldham, Stockport and Wigan for example – whereas the St Louis suburbs are far more residential and middle class. Nor is St Louis circular: the Mississipi river separates the states of Missouri and Illinois, and metropolitan St Louis radiates out in a half-circle on the western bank.

In Manchester the location of hospitals has remained remarkably stable during the radical population shifts of recent decades, but in St Louis many hospitals have relocated to junctions on the ring-road, leaving little more than the two teaching hospitals (Barnes and St Louis University) in the central city. The ten or so hospitals on the ring-road, a mix of for-profit and not-for-profit institutions, compete fiercely for patients in a way unfamiliar to the NHS, even after the introduction of the quasi-market in the 1989–91 reforms.

Finally, within the north west of England the cities of Manchester and, 30 miles to its west, Liverpool vie with one another for the unofficial title 'regional capital', as yet of no constitutional significance though that would change if devolution to regional governments were to be implemented. St Louis, the largest city in Missouri, also has a challenger to its west: 200 miles away, on the other edge of Missouri, lies the large conurbation of Kansas City (the main town, oddly, is in Missouri and not in the State of Kansas). Neither St Louis nor Kansas City is Missouri's state capital: the much smaller Jefferson City, halfway across the state, is the focus of health policy lobbying activity on issues such as Medicaid reform or the regulation of hospitals, doctors and managed care organizations. If Warrington, located midway between Manchester and Liverpool, were to become the centre of a North West Regional Council with responsibility for the NHS, then a further socio-political comparison between the two conurbations would certainly apply. As it happens, it has recently become the location of the NHS Regional Office for the north west.

Within this context, and within the context of the earlier analysis of the extent of patients' association activities and political influence at the national level, this chapter sets the scene by examining the presence of disease-related patients' associations in the two conurbations and by comparing and contrasting their basic organizational features, roles and functions. Chapters 8 and 9 will then analyse in detail their impact in each conurbation.

BRANCHES AND CHAPTERS: PARALLEL UNDERACTIVITY

In both countries the majority of patients' associations have virtually no local structure to them: they are national organizations, often quite small-scale, which operate solely at the national level. Members, supporters and non-members seeking information access them through headquarters, sometimes with the inducement of freephone lines. All income from subscriptions, donations and fund-raising activities goes into the national pot. It is important to be quite clear from the outset that this conurbation comparative case study thus focuses on only a minority of the associations investigated in earlier chapters. That minority may continue to grow as several national associations have ambitions to actively invest resources into regional or local development, often as part of a strategy of moving from all-volunteer to office-based status. But the focus here is on actual levels of local activity in 1997–8, and not on future aspirations.

There is a difference of terminology between the two countries. The local organizations of British national associations are usually styled 'groups' or 'branches' and the latter term will be employed to cover both. In America although the term 'groups' is quite commonly employed, especially in relation to self-help activities, the conventional title for established local organizations, used henceforth, is 'chapter'.

Of the 281 American associations surveyed nationally, just over half (146) claimed to have some kind of a geographical substructure, with the numbers of chapters ranging from only one to several hundred. St Louis' population places it within the fifteen largest American metropolitan areas, and some 101 national associations claimed to have fifteen or more local chapters. Statistically, therefore, there might be expected to be up to about a hundred associations active in St Louis. The fact that after extensive research of local directories, newspapers and other sources only 53 – half the anticipated number – could be identified (and 6 of those had subsequently to be discarded as either moribund, not local or not fulfilling the criteria of patient-focused and disease-related) clearly requires some explanation.

There are two very different possible explanations for this apparent lack of local activity. One is that the national associations overclaim activity. They may include in their numbers every self-help group, however tiny and temporary, whereas the objective of this study was to identify rather more stable organizations. It is noticeable that the use of 'chapter' is avoided by some associations in their returns to directories and encyclopedias, and there was some sign in St Louis suburban newspapers and in hospital leaflets of extremely localized, often hospital-based, support group activity only very tenuously linked to the existence of a national association. However, nowhere near 101 associations or medical conditions can be accounted for in St Louis by adding these instances to the 47 chapters identified as organized and active.

The second possible explanation is that St Louis is underactive. Though large, it lost the title of 'capital of the mid-west' to Chicago many decades ago. With two important exceptions – the massive McDonnell–Douglas Corporation and the Anheuser–Busch brewery – it lacks corporate headquarters of national companies or of public sector associations (both the American Medical and the American Hospitals Associations, for example, are based in Chicago). In short, St Louis lacks the vitality associated with many other giant conurbations (San Francisco, New York, Chicago, Los Angeles, Dallas and so on). It is one of the sleepier big cities, and its political activity matches its place in the American world.

The Greater Manchester experience of patients' association branches offers a crude test of this second explanation. Manchester's reputation is certainly not one of being a sleepy city with below-par political activity, so a larger number of branches than that located in St Louis might be expected. Of the 222 British associations initially identified in the national survey, some 108 claimed to have five or more branches or regional officer arrangements. Yet despite extensive research, no more than 82 associations appeared to be in any way active in Manchester. Some 61 of these had one or more branches in the conurbation. Nine others had a regional office (not necessarily located in the conurbation, nor always covering only the north west), and a further 12 had a 'contact name' of a home-based area officer (in 4 cases the contact point was a hospital clinic).

The figures are not precisely comparable, but it is clear that the activity levels in Manchester are not greatly above those found in St Louis, when one-off self-help groups are added to the 47 chapters. In truth, both seem to underperform. The 'sleepy city' explanation alone is inadequate.

To confirm this initial thesis of underperformance a reverse analysis of British national associations was undertaken. Ten with apparently large memberships and considerable numbers of branches, but with little or no Manchester activity, were identified. In two cases, the National Back Pain Association (61 branches nationally) and the National Meningitis Trust (65 branches), there was just one branch in Manchester. Manchester's 2.7 million population is about 5 per cent of the British total so, statistically, three branches might have been expected. But in the eight other instances there is no scope for any such statistical 'game': there are no Manchester branches at all despite association claims of having significant numbers nationally. These eight include Foresight (the Association for Pre-conceptual Care), with 32 branches elsewhere; the Foundation for the Study of Infant Deaths ('140 plus' branches but 'no groups in the north west'); Headway – National Head Injuries Association (it has 110–115 branches but, even more significant, it runs 40 day care centres – Headway Houses – elsewhere in Britain but not in Manchester); the British Thyroid Foundation ('in the process' of adding a Manchester branch to its other 27); and the Cardiomyopathy Association (whose 20 named 'contacts' included none at all in the whole of the north west region, including Merseyside and Lancashire).

If the core City of Manchester were the focus of this study, a simple explanation might be the difficulty of getting public participation and voluntary activity in an area with a contemporary history of economic decline and with all the other physical and social symptoms conventionally associated with inner city deprivation. The National Back Pain Association had had two branches but the City one 'failed'. Other respondents to the 1997 questionnaire survey remarked on the difficulty of establishing branches in the poorest areas of Manchester. It is indeed the case that the most affluent suburbs lie outside the conurbation, principally in Cheshire. Part of the explanation for Manchester's 'underperformance' is almost certainly class-related. Participation in patients' associations is a middle-class political and social activity: a study of the National Ankylosing Spondylitis Society found that 44 per cent of members were from social classes 1 and 2, with under 10 per cent from classes 4 and 5 (Williams 1989: 144). One likely consequence is that any political influence which associations exert may well favour the middle class.

This thesis has enormous implications for the politics of health, and of patients' associations. It reinforces the notion that needs and supply are in conflict, with the most needy receiving the fewest resources. An alternative snapshot of associations offers some further evidence of this. Thalassaemia and sickle cell disease are inherited blood conditions experienced by the poorest sectors of society: the black and Cypriot communities in particular. In both St Louis and Manchester the patients' associations which support people with these conditions are markedly weak. So financially strapped was the St Louis Metropolitan chapter of the Sickle Cell Disease Association of America that its enthusiastic and caring executive director was personally paying for stamps, envelopes and all other office disposables out of her modest US$18,000 salary. She had no paid help and her board had difficulty in recruiting volunteer members from the surrounding community to serve on it. The shabby offices in a poor, black neighbourhood had been burgled. There was every appearance of a chapter in crisis, running hard in order to stand still, and unable to develop much in the way of either services or organized advice for the 185 known (to her) sufferers in St Louis of this debilitating disease. There were 85 other chapters across the country, but the Californian headquarters boasted a mere six staff so the national level of support for chapters was very limited too.

The UK Thalassaemia Society had no Manchester branch, the nearest being some 25 miles away in Blackburn. (In America the national survey failed to uncover the existence of a specialist thalassaemia association.) At headquarters a tiny core of paid staff remained dependent on volunteers, one of whom acts as unpaid secretary. Since its foundation in 1976 (by the parents of sufferers) it has raised £900,000 for research but it recently spent some of that money simply to 'keep the laboratory open at University College Hospital which would have closed due to lack of [NHS] funds'. A National Lottery Charities Board award of funds for an 'Asian Awareness Campaign' has recently marked a possible upturn in its fortunes, but it had only 606 members in 1997 and it retained its original democratic management system of a fortnightly open committee meeting at its north London base: participative locally maybe, but unlikely to attract any provincial representation from areas like Manchester.

The Sickle Cell Society had several similar characteristics. Founded in 1979 by a group of patients, parents and professional health carers in north west London who shared a 'concern about the lack of understanding and inadequacy of treatment', it too had a tiny core of paid staff but relied heavily on volunteers. By 1995 membership had dwindled to only 75 though a year later this number had risen to 200. Almost moribund, and with both the paid staff ill, it then received three separate charity grants to fund the posts of director, information officer and child development worker, enabling it to become operational again. A small Manchester branch was affiliated to it.

These instances of the struggle to survive, which could be coupled with the observation that there are no known patients' associations in other disease areas prevalent in poor communities (rickets, bronchitis, for example), illustrate the partial coverage of medical conditions. In contrast, conditions like chronic fatigue (ME), repetitive strain injury and eating disorders, all of which have attracted middle-class interest and a consequent aura of respectability, have experienced growing numbers of relatively well-off associations. So, too, have a whole raft of very rare genetic and neurological conditions. The headquarters addresses alone are indicative of the genesis of these associations: 64 of the 170 British associations which responded to the 1997 survey were located in the affluent outer London and south east commuter belt and a further 60 had London postcodes, mostly of their offices in the central area.

SALARIES AND VOLUNTEERISM: CONTRASTING WORLDS

The sharpest organizational difference between Manchester's branches and the St Louis chapters lies in the very basics of their existence. In short, the vast majority of local activity in Britain is through home-based voluntary work whereas the American tradition is to employ salaried officers to lead their chapters.

Only eleven of the 82 British associations active in Manchester had an office (apart from the national headquarters), and 6 of those offices were located outside the Manchester area – 3 in other north western towns and 3 across the Pennines on the eastern side of northern England. At least 5 of the 11 office-based associations either provide mainstream income-generating services such as respite care homes or run chains of charity shops to generate income, and the regional office in those cases constitutes their tier of 'hands-on' middle management. The other 71 associations are all in effect volunteer-led, and contact points are home addresses. In some cases there is a small honorarium paid for part-time work. This applies to a few of the 14 which operate through a regional 'contact' system. A National Lottery award has enabled the National Eczema Society to offer an honorarium of £2000 a year to its 12 new area coordinators, for example. The more local branches, run by 61 associations in Manchester, are all-volunteer organizations.

In 33 of these 61 associations there is only a single branch within the whole of the Manchester conurbation, and 6 of those branches cover a wider area than that. A few meet in hospital clinics or other meeting rooms because the branch is in effect the basis of a self-help group. Most meet in committee members' homes, and most focus on fund-raising activities. There are almost no branch newsletters of the regular type published by national associations, and informal contact by word of mouth is commonplace. Two branches are actually led by residents from the affluent suburbs outside the conurbation, and very few addresses were located in inner city areas: the suburbs provide most of the person-power found in the Manchester branches.

In total contrast, 40 of the 47 St Louis chapters had their own office accommodation and employed at least one salaried executive director, almost all of these being on a full-time basis. (In two other cases, excluded earlier, there proved not to be a local chapter: the local telephone numbers of both the National Osteoporosis Foundation and the Prader–Willi Syndrome Association redirected callers to the headquarters offices, several hundred miles away). Just seven chapters operated in the typical British way of all-volunteer committees meeting mainly in members' homes. Four of those seven were interviewed: two of the local volunteer spokespeople (for the International Rett Syndrome Association and the Tourette Syndrome Association) had as high priority the aim of establishing their own offices when (or if) finances allowed.

It should not be inferred from this that voluntary work for patients' associations is a British monopoly. Rather, the contrast represents a different tradition in America which runs right across the health sector. All hospitals, whether they be for-profit, or not-for-profit, utilize very large numbers of volunteers who work in almost every department to enhance service quality. So do most of the 40 patients' association chapters, especially for fund-raising and for routine office work. But the American approach has long been to 'manage' these volunteers professionally: one professional sub-group within the American Hospitals Association, for example, is that for directors of volunteers and it has around 2000 members for whom there are all the usual courses and conferences, and who can seek fellowship status through study and research. There is a professional association for charity officers too, but only one executive director interviewed mentioned being a member.

Although numbers are growing steadily in Britain, very few hospitals have properly integrated management of their volunteers, many of whom are recruited by separate voluntary bodies (like the Red Cross) which offer an in-hospital service as one part of their overall activities. Likewise only a few of the very largest patients' associations have professional management at the sub-national level. Sometimes that management is to oversee directly provided services and shops, clearly essential to ensure quality and to monitor efficiency and effectiveness. Occasionally it is to recruit and train volunteer workers, as in the case of the large mental illness charities (and of some disability groups, which lay beyond the scope of this study).

BOARDS AND COMMITTEES: STRENGTHS AND WEAKNESSES

The sharp Manchester–St Louis contrast extends to the management and oversight of officials. Manchester branches are run by committees of association members, with the volunteer officers responsible in effect to their 'peers'. Committee members bring with them support and commitment, important philanthropic attributes. They commonly have, or have had, hands-on experience of the particular condition which the association targets, as either patients, relatives or carers. They are frequently recruited by existing branch officials, by word of mouth. They form a tight-knit group of friends, and committees are small, usually less than ten strong.

The handful of all-volunteer St Louis chapters follow this same pattern, but the 40 office-based chapters operate very differently. As American associations graduate to established status they take on some of the trappings of the American corporation: in particular the title of executive director and the concept of a board. The board is made up of unpaid non-executive directors who hold career posts elsewhere. Board members are recruited from a range of community interests: industrial and commercial companies, public sector bodies, and sometimes health care provider or payer organizations. Although they are most unlikely to serve unless they have a degree of broad support for the goals of the association and chapter, most are not active volunteer workers in the way that the all-volunteer committee members of home-based chapters and of British branches tend to be.

Chapter boards are also quite large. The St Louis Alzheimer's

Association chapter had 26 members in 1996–7, when it employed 25 salaried staff and claimed to have 3000–4000 members. One of the smallest boards, with only 10 members (even so, bigger than most Manchester branch committees), was that of the Huntington's Disease Society chapter, whose offices were open for only fourteen hours a week. But size of board was not necessarily always related to chapter size or activity: there were 22 on the Amyotrophic Lateral Sclerosis (motor neurone disease) board, although the chapter has but one employee working in office-space donated by, and located within, a factory; 21 directors of the (barely larger) Alliance for the Mentally Ill; and 28 of the (two staff) National Neurofibromatosis Foundation chapter, for example. Some reasons for this size of board, including the possible use of boards to forge relationships with health care providers and payers, will be examined in more detail in Chapter 8.

This Anglo-American contrast of management arrangements has three important consequences for chapter and branch activity. These relate to internal accountability, expectations and representation. First, the most obvious weakness of the all-volunteer committee of peers, meeting in someone's home, is that it generates an atmosphere of social friendship which militates against robust monitoring and accountability. Few Manchester branches or St Louis all-volunteer chapters appeared to have any clear targets or strategic objectives, for example, in contrast to their office-based equivalents. Indeed, many were struggling to survive at all, commonly citing the difficulty of getting any members to join 'the committee' or to fill key posts such as secretary and treasurer. And it is not clear whether these committees contain members who are basically questioning, even sceptical: an attribute of most effective committees. The co-option of businesspeople and other public persons on to chapter boards of directors heightens accountability as the executive director has to produce regular activity reports and to answer to experienced managers from beyond the charity world.

The second consequence follows directly from this. Levels of expectations differ. The chapter executive director operates in an environment in which there is pressure to match the expectations of efficiency and effectiveness which board members bring with them. This is both a questioning and an ideas-based environment, and it contrasts with the modest expectations of many volunteer committee members, often themselves experiencing the medical condition which the association represents and consequently often experiencing life through the eyes of the grateful recipient of health care services. Thus every board member of the all-volunteer, home-based National Sjogren's Syndrome Association's chapter had the condition, and the chapter president's limited expectations stemmed from her perception that this is 'a low-key illness of older folk which generates little public sympathy'.

The third consequence relates to the association's ability to represent the needs of people with a particular medical condition. Effective interaction with health agencies and institutions requires not just skills of communication and negotiation but also the key political resource of legitimacy. The seemingly 'amateurish' association has less chance of gaining access to health policy makers because it gives out negative signals: one British study of mental health groups indicates that because they do not operate bureaucratically like the bodies they seek to influence, this can be used by policy makers to de-legitimize them (Harrison *et al.* 1997).

This all suggests that there are advantages in operating through an arm's-length board. But against this there is the important argument that such boards are 'out of touch' because they have little or no personal experience of the medical condition which the association seeks to represent. They may consequently have unrealistic expectations of what can be achieved, and of the basic practical needs of people with a particular condition. In practice, some boards do include representative members, and all have medical expert members or a separate medical advisory committee. In addition, to overcome this potential knowledge gap, many American office-based chapters have both a board of directors and, separately, some form of a patients' (or parents') forum or committee. This dual approach of separating management from user representation has the benefit of enhancing both external accountability and internal arrangements to ensure that salaried officers are in touch with members' needs and aspirations. The 'typical' all-volunteer home-based branches in Manchester, and the small number of similar but 'untypical' St Louis chapters, lack this dual approach. Consequently their external stimulus is limited locally, and their accountability systems are at best variable in their robustness.

Finally, the arm's-length board may fail either to monitor activity adequately or even to continue to exist. The National Neurofibromatosis Foundation's chapter, for example, became virtually moribund when vacancies were not filled due to organizational inertia. Eventually board membership dropped to only three. Intervention from the national headquarters resulted in a change of executive director (the previous person has since left another local chapter of a different association) with a remit to revive the chapter which she was actively pursuing. Board enlargement to 28 members was accompanied by a new medical advisory board and a separate celebrity advisory board. A 70 per cent increase in income in the first year of the new regime resulted. In this case, near-failure had led to successful regeneration: in contrast, however, the Prader–Willi Syndrome Association had closed down.

CONCLUSIONS

This chapter has provided an initial overview of local activity in Manchester and St Louis, and has offered several explanations of the apparent lack, in both conurbations, of patients' association activity, relative to nationwide population-based norms. A thesis of class-related activity levels emerged as a strong explanatory variable, with wider consequences for the distributional politics of health. Also highlighted has been the enormous difference in basic organizational arrangements: the American preference for local activity based on offices and salaried officials contrasts sharply with British norms of all-volunteer branches.

Almost certainly there has emerged an impression that the overwhelming contrast is between American 'professionalism' and British 'amateurism', and that professionalism may have the advantage in offering a more effective organization. That is the orthodox American view – hence most St Louis chapters have their own offices and salaried staff, and those that do not, usually aspire to so do. Very different circumstances apply in Manchester, with paid officials and office space a rarity. The stereotyped branch officer is a part-time 'amateur', working for the association from home in their own spare time, and apparently lacking much in the way of back-up support from any sub-national or regional infrastructure.

That impression needs now to be put firmly to the test. Are office-based chapters really as effective as this picture implies? Are branches actually weak and unstable organizations, lacking in resources? Is there clearly a 'best way' of organizing associations locally? These questions provide the basic framework for detailed studies of each conurbation in the next two chapters. The approach will be one of scepticism about the possibility that any one particular organizational arrangement can be markedly superior to any other. Questions are addressed about the composition and roles of executive directors and boards; about the extent to which volunteerism is utilized in both countries; about the vitality or otherwise of volunteer-run branches in Manchester; about relationships between chapters/branches and headquarters; about local interassociational links; and about the nature of local activity in the two conurbations (the relative importance of support, services and fund-raising in particular). Just how strong are the apparently active St Louis chapters, and how vulnerable to inactivity and closure are the Manchester branches?

8

ST LOUIS – LOCAL STRENGTH?

In Chapter 7 it was noted that 53 associations apparently active in St Louis (the metropolitan area) were initially identified; that six were quickly discarded as not fitting the criteria for this study; and that 40 of the remaining 47 were office-based organizations with salaried staff.

The six discarded were two which had no medical or clinical focus (they centred on social care); one which had closed down (allegedly the national headquarters of the Prader–Willi Syndrome Association – calls were diverted to a Los Angeles number of a managed care organization, and the executive director had been fired); two others which proved to be local telephone numbers only, with calls automatically diverted to offices elsewhere (San Francisco in the case of the National Alopecia Areata Foundation and Washington DC for the National Osteoporosis Foundation); and one (the association representing people with hydrocephalus) which just could not be contacted, even over several weeks. The remaining 47 were contacted with requests for literature and 23 were interviewed during October–November 1997.

Because the key aim of this chapter is to analyse the strengths and weaknesses of the office-based, salaried staff model of local activity, the focus is on the 40 such chapters surveyed in St Louis, of which 19 were visited and interviewed. The seven home-based, all-volunteer chapters (four interviewed) are reviewed with the Manchester branches in Chapter 9.

The 40 was reduced to 39 by excluding the Kilo Diabetes and Vascular Research Foundation. This had every appearance of being a patients' association: a board of directors, newsletter, seminars; fund-raising events, but it had been founded in 1972 by two doctors as a source of charitable finance for their laboratory: Dr Kilo remains chairman of the board and director of clinical research (three other Kilo names are listed too), and his co-founder, Dr Williamson is still director of laboratory research. This patently did not meet the study's criterion of 'patient-led, required for inclusion.

Semi-structured interviews, lasting from 50 to 90 minutes, were annotated, not taped, and Association literature was reviewed. Despite arrangements being made through 'cold' telephone calls, no executive director refused an interview; nor did any refuse to respond to particular questions: invaluable total cooperation and courtesy was experienced. This reflected both a natural curiosity on their part (not one cited having previously been the subject of any academic interest, let alone from a British researcher) and also their commitment to, and commendable pride in, their work as managers of charitable and philanthropic activity.

Much of what follows is narrative material on the organization and activities of office-based chapters in St Louis, with some on-going assessment of strengths and weaknesses. Continuing themes will be those of coping with increasing competition in a more and more crowded 'marketplace' for both volunteerism and fund-raising; the turfist nature of chapters and lack of coalition activity; the cost-effectiveness of some activities in an era of competitive contracts; and the generally very limited links which they appear to have with local or state-level health policy makers, payers or providers. In short, research indicates that there is marked potential for associations both to operate more effectively and to increase their influence over health care provision in St Louis.

STRUCTURE AND AUTONOMY

Executive director and of board of directors are titles used virtually universally across all 39 chapters (one was styled president, another two were coordinators). This masks much variation in practice over two important issues: the extent to which accountability arrangements are determined locally or laid down nationally by the parent association; and the frequency and, more particularly, the nature of board/executive director interaction.

National/local relationships are of two contrasting types. Twelve of the nineteen St Louis chapters interviewed have boards which appoint their own staff and enjoy devolved power akin to a federal system of government, albeit often with model structures and by-laws emanating from the centre. This devolution contrasts sharply with six other chapters whose constitutions place them as the agent of the parent association. Under this centralized model the executive director is appointed by, and is accountable through, line management either direct to national headquarters or to an intermediate 'regional' tier of management, with the chapter board seeking to exert influence without power. It has 'a consulting and assisting remit' stated one executive director; it 'fund-raises and monitors quality' said another; while a third felt it 'could raise some commotion' if unhappy with his or her performance. The nineteenth, the American Parkinson Disease Association (PDA), also has a board limited to advisory functions: the chapter 'coordinator' works in a specialist referral centre and is employed by the University Medical School. She initiated the chapter in the late 1980s, when her advertisement proposing a support group led 350 people to attend a public meeting. By 1997 PDA had over 25 such groups running in St Louis.

There was no clear relationship between chapter autonomy and the intensity of board-level activity. Some boards met monthly, but most were bimonthly or quarterly, though almost always with a form of executive committee in between. Executive directors sometimes had to circulate a written report for every meeting, but a small number were permitted to operate mostly through verbal reports, which seemed surprising. Two extremes were the Muscular Dystrophy Association (MDA) with a regional officer both hiring and firing chapter executive directors and requiring a weekly report, especially on fund-raising; and the (devolved) ALS Association (motor neurone disease) whose board meets just five times a year without routinely requiring written reports from the executive director. Interestingly, in cases of centralized management like MDA the local literature makes no mention of this, because to highlight the fact that fund-raising income is not distributed locally might deter would-be donors and volunteer workers.

Cases like ALS (one of several with low-key boards) were doubly surprising. First, boards of directors are quite different entities from the type of all-volunteer committees of members and supporters to be examined in Chapter 9. As noted in Chapter 7, boards are consciously recruited from the business and professional communities as well as the caring and health management sectors, to give an image of purpose and calibre. One might expect attorneys, accountants and senior corporate managers, however supportive they are of the association's mission, to demand regular written reports on progress towards agreed targets and strategies. That clearly is not always the case. Yet, secondly, this is despite a widely held view that the not-for-profit sector has problems in attracting high calibre managers because pay levels are often modest and there is no clear career structure. One executive director spoke of her opposite numbers (if not of herself) thus: 'most of them are in it because they can't get jobs elsewhere'.

This extreme comment masks the fact that several executive directors interviewed were clearly both highly motivated and very talented managers. It does, however, supplement the second reason why boards might be expected to monitor performance closely: the high turnover of executive directors, whether through resignation or dismissal, is striking. From interviews it probably reflects a combination of varied calibre, modest salaries and different backgrounds which do not necessarily ensure skills in the management of office-based activity (many of the executive directors had come from jobs such as teaching, social work, residential care, youth groups and leisure work).

Short stays were widely perceived by interviewees as both commonplace and inevitable in the not-for-profit sector. One, who had joined the National Society for Fundraising Executives (NSFE), referred to a recent NSFE survey showing the average tenure of charity fund-raisers as only about eighteen months. Only five of the nineteen executive directors interviewed had been in post for as long as seven years and five others were very new (less than a year). Of the latter, one reported that her predecessor had left under a cloud and had already departed from another association; a second that in the sixteen-year history of the chapter no executive director had yet lasted for as long as two years. A third chose not to mention that her predecessor had been summarily dismissed.

Most of those new in post had inherited problems of chapter inactivity. In the case of the National Neurofibromatosis Foundation, for example, the board of directors had shrunk to only three members and the chapter was 'near-moribund': in Chapter 7 it was noted that the spiral of decline had been reversed in this case. The Asthma and Allergy Foundation was another in some disarray. It had no newsletter, held only two sizeable fund-raising events in 1996, and its new incumbent was 'trying to revitalize' the educational programme: all four of the chapter staff were newly in post and highly motivated but were also clearly in need of board direction and support because both of the enthusiastic senior managers had been salaried careworkers and came with no experience of charity or general management.

CHAPTER SIZE

Associations nationally vary greatly in their scale, as noted in Chapter 3. So do their local chapters, even when (as here) attention is focused only on those with offices and salaried staff. Two measures of the extent of this variation are staffing levels and financial turnover.

Eleven of the nineteen chapters interviewed were small-scale offices, with fewer than five paid staff: several had just the executive director and an assistant. Four others had between five and ten staff, and three others were of a very similar size, all with between 18 and 25 employees (American Lung Association; Alzheimer's Association; National Multiple Sclerosis Society). The nineteenth was very different, and clearly the outlier: the giant United Cerebral Palsy Association chapter, in effect a major not-for-profit service provider, employed no fewer than 135 rehabilitation and office-based staff.

These figures complete only part of the picture. As might be expected, given the mission and philanthropic nature of chapters, paid staff are frequently supplemented by office-based volunteers. Here there was again much variation. Unexpectedly, many small chapters with only one or two salaried employees made little or no use of volunteers for office work. In contrast the larger ones (though not United Cerebral Palsy) utilized a good deal of unpaid office labour. The Lung Association and the Leukemia Society of America both had four or five voluntary office workers every day. Alzheimer's Association had even more. It boasted up to 650 volunteers in all, but most are involved in fund-raising, support groups and other programmes, discussed in the next section, rather than in office work. The (ten staff) Epilepsy Foundation claimed to utilize around 250 volunteers across its activities; the Alliance for the Mentally Ill about 80 to 90. In contrast, the Asthma and Allergy Foundation had just one office volunteer; the Sickle Cell Disease Association (one paid staff) had only two.

Financially the eighteen chapters providing data (one chose not to do so) fall into two distinct groupings. Seven are million dollar bodies, with incomes ranging from US$1.5 million to US$3.0

million in fiscal year 1996–7. In contrast, nine others had turnovers of below US$300,000, leaving just two at around the half-million mark. The correlation with staff numbers is far from significant as an important variable here is the focus of the association. The 'whole mission' of the Juvenile Diabetes Foundation (JDF), for example, is fund-raising for research. One of the smallest in staff numbers (three paid employees), its annual income of US$476,000 placed it at the median financially. Research funding is also a high priority for the American Diabetes Association, though unlike JDF it has a range of local programmes too. Its fund-raising activity gave it a US$2.9 million income despite it employing only seven staff. This was only US$100,000 below the turnover of the giant United Cerebral Palsy Association.

The poor relations emerge all too clearly from this simple financial analysis. With a mere US$22,000 income, the Sickle Cell Disease Association struggles to meet the office rent and a single salary: it exists on a budget little bigger than that of the all-volunteer Spina Bifida Association chapter or of the Huntington's Disease Society, whose chapter office opens for only 14 hours a week. In addition, SCDA has difficulty in attracting volunteers or raising funds or obtaining corporate sponsors in a poor, black neighbourhood. The Alliance for the Mentally Ill (US$176,000) also enjoys (or endures) modest finances, though volunteer recruitment has been easier since it was finally able, only in 1990, to move from all-volunteer to salaried, office-based.

These two cases illustrate the way in which certain conditions, including Alzheimer's, diabetes and leukaemia, become labelled as fashionable, acceptable or respectable, with financial and staffing consequences as a result. In America the first and last of these have personally affected two recent presidents, Reagan and Bush (who lost a child to leukaemia), and their support for these causes has had a major impact. Celebrity support has helped other causes such as motor neurone disease, nicknamed 'Lou Gehrig's disease' after the famous baseball player, but other conditions, including sickle cell disease and mental illness, have largely missed out, and not only in St Louis. The future of the Sickle Cell chapter is particularly parlous: no less than 75 per cent of its tiny income in 1996–7 was from a single source – the Combined Health Appeal (of which more below), and the Appeal's policy is to expect its contributions to be at least matched by other donations and corporate sponsorships. This general issue of disease status is further considered in Chapter 10, p. 190.

SERVICES AND ACTIVITIES

The mission of patients' associations is, of course, to provide much more than jobs for officials. Whether it be 'Support–Education–Advocacy–Research' (Alliance for the Mentally Ill), 'Public Education and Fundraising' (Cystic Fibrosis Foundation) or 'Fighting 40 Neuromuscular Diseases' (Muscular Dystrophy Association), most have slogans and more detailed objectives by which they can be judged. In the above cases, for instance, it can be concluded that the Alliance contributes little if anything towards research as provision of its services dominates its extremely limited financial and human resources, and that the Foundation's literature offered no evidence of public education services: it, in effect, focused solely on fund-raising.

This study does not seek to quantify and compare chapter performance with any precision. The St Louis office-based chapters instead provide scope for broad evaluation of the 'added value' of employing paid staff and operating from a working office. This can then be compared in Chapter 9 with the alternative home-based all-volunteer model. Here the evidence sought reflects the hypotheses of the office model: that levels of activity will be high because of the established nature of the local organization; and that executive directors can both do more themselves and achieve more from subordinates and volunteers through good management than might be achieved by volunteers alone. Some statistical data are often available but, in the end, evaluation inevitably has to reflect judgement. There is no precise 'control group' here, and the all-volunteer associations examined in Chapter 9 have too few resources to be truly comparable organizations. Indeed it is only lack of resources that prevents the American ones from establishing a salaried office in line with the prevailing culture of not-for-profits that the office is an important indicator of life and activity. Is this really the case?

The evidence examined below is patchy. There are vibrant, successful local chapters achieving a great deal. By this is meant that they provide the management infrastructure which facilitates or supports a wide range of activities. But there are others which do little more than routine administrative work with little evidence of significant activities to support members. For ease of analysis, chapter activities are analysed under three heads: those supporting individuals with particular conditions; those targeting health professionals through the provision of education and training in the particular needs of people with the condition(s) the association represents; and fund-raising to increase research into cures or the alleviation of those conditions (this study necessarily excludes consideration of the effectiveness of that research: chapters raise funds, and that is the measure of their success).

Supportive activities

Supportive activities include the provision of support or self-help groups and of information and advice, often through helplines. Evidence of 'value-added' is clearest when the paid staff of the chapter undertake actions that multiply provision. They, for example, help a support group become established by finding a venue, assisting with publicity, and training leaders. In this respect the history of the American Parkinson Disease Association (with 1.5 paid staff), cited above, offers evidence of real achievement: within a decade it grew from running a single support group to providing the infrastrusture for such groups to operate at 21 venues, with speech therapy sessions at two others, and a further six exercise classes (about ten of these take place within the conurbation: the chapter's geographical remit extends more widely). In the two months of October–November 1997 the Alliance for the Mentally Ill calendar included 34 meetings of its 20 or so support groups and social activities, all 'peer or professionally led', many on a voluntary basis. The helpline, 'manned by trained volunteers', answered 1366 calls in 1996. Their analysis indicated that 53 per cent came from worried families and that half related to a list of very serious conditions, headed by schizophrenia (244 calls alone).

The much bigger Alzheimer's Association (AA) has equally impressive figures: over 80 support groups, with one or more in 32 of the 37 counties it covers (counties are very small areas in Missouri); a helpline receiving 10,000 calls a year and manned by over 20 trained volunteers, and in all some 600 active voluntary workers on its programmes. Like many hospitals, AA 'costs' the value of volunteers: in October 1997, for example, '458 donated 2385 hours of service'. At a hypothetical rate of US$5 an hour this equates to almost US$150,000 a year. The smaller Epilepsy Foundation reported that in 1996 its volunteers (about 250 of them) 'provided 9847 hours of service'. The National Multiple Sclerosis Society had 35 volunteer-led support groups, eight of them in St Louis (it also covers a wider area), and 90 of its trained leaders attended its annual leadership skills refresher course. The tiny (two paid staff)

Lupus Foundation of America chapter answered 5000 queries in 1996 and had six active support groups. These six chapters provided impressive evidence to demonstrate proven potential. With good management, added value can be obtained. It has to be said, however, that by no means all the office-based chapters can offer similar evidence, whether it be of support groups, helplines or other supportive services or activities of their choice. As with the six more active chapters, the examples are indicative rather than comprehensive, and comparable evidence from other chapters could also be cited.

Two bodies compete for coverage of motor neurone disease, in St Louis and nationally. The ALS Association chapter has only one support group which meets in its offices but was 'not very flourishing'. Beyond that there was 'no real outreach – yet', but activity in other directions did include equipment loan (favourably commented on by its competitor) and the employment of a social worker offering counselling, though whether, at a cost of US$30,000 annually, this constituted 'added value' is debatable. The much larger Muscular Dystrophy Association (MDA) also lists ALS as a condition it represents (and both bodies freely use pictures of Lou Gehrig in baseball action in their publicity). One of its three (only) support groups is specifically for people and families experiencing ALS, but the facilitator is paid to lead it. Few other MDA service programmes appear to target ALS (fund-raising apart, considered below separately). Although MDA does refer people in need of equipment to the ALS Association, the two in no way collaborate and MDA pointed out that it predated the ALS Association, implying that the latter had chosen to compete. That neither makes any mention of the other in its literature reflects the competitive quest for 'market share': the same process of ignoring the presence of competitors applies equally in the cases of conditions such as asthma and lung, lupus, and arthritis.

There are other instances of unimpressive support service activity. The Asthma and Allergy Foundation, cited earlier as 'trying to revitalize' on the appointment of four new staff, had a helpline and a 'Project Concern' offering cash aid and aimed at children needing drugs and equipment, but no support group following the failure of one in 1995. The virtually moribund chapter of the National Neurofibromatosis Foundation, though developing under new leadership, had no support groups in 1997 although there were aspirations to establish two.

Professional education and training

The intensity of professional education and training activity was equally variable. The American Lung Association, for example, held just 'one or two' annual seminars for nurses, and a single dinner for physicians (with a visiting speaker, to attract them) – hardly an intensive programme of activity. The Crohn's and Colitis Foundation offered physicians a one-day course which had been externally accredited for medical training, as well as a dinner event, but it as yet only had aspirations about offering a programme for nurses. Annual medical symposia were quite common, with well known guest speakers to attract attendance, though this still varied from only 20 or so to a hundred or more (more than 5000 doctors are in practice in St Louis).

A very different approach to professional education was being attempted by the innovative executive director of the National Multiple Sclerosis Society chapter: take to and show a hospital (its managers, physicians, nurses and therapists) a model programme of care, at no cost, in the hope that the hospital would choose to adopt it. Another method was to design and distribute information packs: the National Neurofibromatosis Foundation was about to circulate one to all 13,000 physicians in Missouri, and several other chapters had done likewise. The Alzheimer's Association (AA) was focusing on nurses and it had competed with other providers of training to have courses accepted in the Missouri League for Nursing training catalogue (amazingly, one of the chapter's competitors was its own national association). It had been targeting nursing homes in particular as there were public concerns about care standards, and it offered tailor-made short courses, for which it was beginning to charge a fee to the home-owners. One of the most active in the training field, AA's activities placed the more modest performance of others into some perspective, though it must be recalled that the Association had 25 paid staff and thus was one of the largest chapter offices in St Louis.

Fund-raising

Evaluating fund-raising efforts is equally problematic, for two reasons. First, causes vary in their public image and it is easier to obtain donations and corporate sponsorship for some than it is for others. Second, staff inputs again vary, with the larger offices employing specialized salaried fund-raisers and the smaller ones relying on their generic managers. Occasionally there are direct comparisons. Two chapters, of the Muscular Dystrophy Association and the Juvenile Diabetes Foundation, each employed three-person teams of fund-raisers: they raised US$625,000 and US$476,000 respectively in 1996–7. The slightly smaller American Lung Association (ALA, 2.5 fund-raisers) raised around US$900,000 but the chapter accounts showed unusually high overheads of around US$375,000. Unfortunately, ALAs accounts, unlike most others, did not separate out fund-raising expenses from general management costs.

Inevitably the less popular diseases received least support. The Sickle Cell Disease Association raised only about US$5000 in 1996–7, but not for want of effort. It was noted earlier that this condition, with its prevalence amongst the poorest groups in society, attracts little public interest or support. The Alliance for the Mentally Ill raised US$40,000 from its 'special events', but these cost US$13,000 to stage. The contrast in scale with the American Diabetes Association (ADA) is stark, though the ratio of costs to income is fairly similar: ADA raised a massive US$952,000 from its special events, spending US$297,000 on all fund-raising activities in the process.

These so-called special events range from large-scale sponsored walks, runs and fishing events through golf tournaments (arguably hardly 'special': one interviewee had calculated that about 600 charity golf tournaments for not-for-profit bodies take place in St Louis every summer) to glamorous balls and dinners. The Asthma and Allergy Foundation (AAF), for example, raised US$161,000, more than half of its total annual income of US$298,000, from just two such events: a golf tournament and a ball, at a combined cost of some US$40,000. Such sums come largely through commercial sponsorship and support, a marked feature of most chapters' fund-raising activity, and a particular target for AAF as asthma is universally prevalent in workforces and is perceived by the middle class as 'respectable' and hence worthy of support. Although most events are local, some coincide nationally with nominated disease weeks, and sometimes there is a major national event which chapters utilize. The annual Jerry Lewis Telethon in support of the Muscular Dystrophy Association is perhaps the best known of these: the chapter raised just over US$1 million that single day in 1997 (nationwide, MDA benefited by about US$50 million).

In all three cases – support services, professional education and fund-raising – the evidence of achievement has been extremely variable. Some excellent work is clearly going on (and space precludes full coverage, particularly in the area of support where a wide range of different initiatives emerged), but other chapters are off the pace of the best. What is apparent is that office-based salaried chapters do have the *potential* to develop services, education and fund-raising in ways that all-volunteer bodies cannot hope to match: they can invest their resources to work intensively on projects supported by the necessary managerial back-up. There is, however, no guarantee that the gap between potential and actual activity levels will always be bridged.

LIAISON AND COLLABORATION

Collaborative activity has several theoretical attractions. These include the cost-effectiveness of sharing office overheads, services or programmes; the scope for greater public impact of large fund-raising or health promotional events marketed and run jointly; and the potential political impact of coalition strategies to alter public policies. However, in Chapter 5 the culture of 'turfism' amongst national associations was identified and in Chapter 6 the lack of political alliances was uncovered, particularly in America. Not surprisingly, therefore, at the chapter level in St Louis the reality is that there is extreme reluctance to collaborate.

There are occasions when an appearance of joint working is present. Several associations will have displays at health fairs, for example, though with separate stands (there are occasional examples of the smallest chapters sharing here). In 1997, six associations went further and organized a joint programme of seminars for carers. Attendance was disappointing, but much more significant for this study were the interview responses of executive directors: conflicting accounts were offered about which of the six chapters did and did not 'pull their weight'.

The reality is that every chapter values its autonomy, sees itself as in competition for market share with other not-for-profits, and so signs up to the dominant culture of pluralist capitalism. What one termed 'the usual territorial culture' prevails. Thus nationally the Lupus Foundation of America had just merged with the American Lupus Society: this had greatly surprised the executive director of the Foundation's local chapter who, like other interviewees, roundly declared 'we all treat each other as competitors'. Other comments along similar lines included 'monopolies just aren't American'; and 'when appointed I was told to compete with the Lung Association and my board opposes ideas of shared resources'. Although two interviewees (of nineteen) did express some feeling that change might be beneficial, and although there is a tiny handful of examples of collaboration, it is clear that significant change would need to come from external stimuli – the other 17 executive directors had refused to be drawn at all on the subject despite being questioned directly. Three possible stimuli, considered here in turn, are market forces, health care reforms and cooperative fund-raising.

Market forces

Market forces might stimulate change. Rapidly rising numbers of not-for-profit organizations (in fields as diverse as health, welfare, housing, the environment, culture, animal welfare) compete for support (funds, volunteer labour) in a marketplace which is growing more crowded and whose capacity for continued expansion is unclear. In health care alone, for example, half the patients' associations in America were found in Chapter 3 to be less than 20 years old. Several chapter executive directors in St Louis openly admitted that fund-raising was becoming an increasing challenge. Some chapter accounts confirmed this: in 1995–6, for example, the American Lung Association saw its chapter income from donations, direct mail appeals and special events fall by 10 per cent, from US$952,000 to US$857,000, despite its employing a team of 2.5 full-time equivalent dedicated fund-raisers. Others were finding it hard to recruit good volunteers to supplement their paid staff. But, barring a serious ongoing economic recession, the increasingly crowded marketplace seemed, of itself, unlikely to stimulate more than very marginal change: the culture of turfism is far too deeply embedded for that to happen.

Health care reforms

Responding to, or even initiating, health care reforms might also stimulate change. Access to care and cost containment policies have been high on the American political agenda in the 1990s and they remain key public policy concerns, despite the failure of the Clinton Plan in 1992–4. Just as nationally, chapters too should have strong interests in both access and cost issues: after all, they claim to represent many who are beneficiaries of government Medicare and Medicaid programmes.

By good fortune, the 19 interviews of executive directors were held in the immediate months after two very important State of Missouri policy debates. One related to the application to the federal government for a 'Medicaid waiver' to allow Missouri to expand coverage to 154,000 additional beneficiaries who lacked health insurance; the other was the passage of legislation regulating the activities of HMOs (managed care organizations) in the interests of patients. Both items potentially had great significance for consumers of health care.

As charities, patients' associations have political restrictions and cannot actively campaign on behalf of any individual politician without jeopardizing their tax benefits. However, they are allowed to undertake 'advocacy' and this is interpreted to cover collective causes as well as individual patient cases and entitlements. Some chapters did participate in the debates by, for example, giving evidence at public hearings held by the state's legislative committee on the draft HMO bill, or by urging supporters to write to their elected representatives. In Chapter 6, examples of chapters maintaining databases for letter-writing campaigns were given: the Alzheimer's Association, for example, had about 1100 names, all coded by their local, state and national elected representatives, who could be circulated with a draft lobbying letter. What was striking, however, was that the chapters interviewed had made no attempt to act in concert on either the Medicaid waiver or the HMO bill.

The Medicaid waiver had been under consideration in the Missouri Department of Health since 1994. That year a body styled Missouri Consumer Health Care Watch was founded to oppose the original draft because it 'lacked consumer protection'. By 1997, Watch had 80 organizations in membership, almost all of them volunteer bodies in the welfare field. Funds had been raised (including a grant from Kellogg's) and an office established. Watch lobbied actively on the waiver and also gave evidence in public in 1996 on the draft HMO bill. However, despite 'health' being its remit and title, not a single patients' association interviewed for this study had joined (one not interviewed – Paraquad – was listed and represented on the thirteen-member steering committee). Only one interviewee even mentioned Watch's existence, although it was publishing a good regular newsletter and its office was in St Louis (very near to several of the chapters surveyed here, as it happens). The chair of Watch planned to target patients' associations to further increase membership, in view of their near total absence. She may find success elusive because the turfist culture encourages most executive directors to adopt an introverted approach to Watch.

Cooperative fund-raising

Cooperative fund-raising has a history dating back to the last years of the nineteenth century in America (although it never caught on in Britain). Given the culture of turfism today, it is interesting to note that the origins of this cooperation lay 'in an effort to remove what was seen as the destructive competitiveness between different charities in their annual fundraising drives' (Ware 1989: 131). The two main institutions, United Way and the Combined Health Appeal, were briefly introduced in Chapter 5.

The major cooperative fund-raiser of the two is United Way. In St Louis, as in every other metropolitan area across America, its annual high-profile campaign, launched simultaneously on every TV channel and lasting for some two months, focuses on a combination of corporate donations and payroll deductions. There is no doubting United Way's financial success. In 1997 some 140 organizations around the St Louis area shared in the outcome, with more than US$40 million distributed. However, only 10 of the 47 disease-related patients' associations identified for this study were direct beneficiaries (obtaining well under US$4 million, or less than 10 per cent of the total) and criticism that the United Way movement has a tendency to support safe, respectable charities (Ware 1989: 133) is perhaps borne out by the fact that well over half the St Louis distribution to health charities went to the 'big three': the local chapters of the cancer, heart and lung associations. True these are the major killer diseases but many other chapters are active in those areas or in other areas where the prevalence of disease is also high. A further indication that United Way has a limited health focus is that its 1996 community service directory of over 900 bodies 'that provide an established and continuing array of health and human services' failed to list no fewer than 13 of the 47 patients' associations identified by this study. Finally, no interviewee offered any evidence of United Way attempting to influence chapters to cooperate in any way beyond their brief involvement in the annual campaign.

Across America a move to establish a competitor to United Way, focusing solely on health-related charities, emerged in the 1970s. By 1997 the Combined Health Appeal (CHA) of America had over 40 local chapters including one covering Greater St Louis, established in 1988. Though, as the CHA executive director put it, 'the two are at odds with one another', within a year an agreement between the two was reached to avoid competing annual campaigns, and about half the income which CHA now generates comes from its participation in the United Way campaign (US$910,000 of the US$2 million total CHA budget in 1997). A third competitor, the National Voluntary Health Agencies (NVHA) has a handful of St Louis patients' associations in membership but NVHA lacked a local chapter or any proper cooperative activity (in 1997 it was in talks nationally with CHA about a possible merger).

Unlike United Way, the CHA's potential significance in stimulating joint working goes well beyond fund-raising. CHA organizes health fairs, offers facilities for chapter board meetings and for their support groups where they lack adequate offices of their own, and encourages fresh thinking about shared resources if not outright mergers. Fourteen of the fifteen 1997 members of CHA were patients' associations already included in this study (the fifteenth, the St Louis Society for Children and Adults with Physical Disabilities, was outwith the criteria because its focus was social welfare rather than health), though several other all-volunteer home-based chapters were also affiliated to CHA (and given free use of its meeting facilities).

Full membership of CHA had strings attached, both financial and managerial: executive directors had to attend monthly meetings and contribute dues in order to benefit later from distributions, and the (new in 1997) CHA executive director had embarked on a cost-efficiency policy. His vision was of shared facilities (a building, one receptionist, pooled office technology, and so on) across the smaller associations. Every monthly meeting of executive directors included an agenda item 'Save the Dollar' for the exchange of ideas on economy and efficiency, and all executive directors were being required to undertake a 'management audit' at the time of interviews. The CHA aim was to compare costs such as office rents, proportions of budgets spent on administration and fund-raising, and (through completion of 'time sheets' over a month) apportionment of executive directors' time to various tasks. This was all designed to contribute to the main agenda of collaboration, a policy directly reflecting the CHA executive director's previous personal experience: he had worked for a year in the tiny chapter office of a member association and had felt it to be neither cost-effective nor a stimulus to innovation.

Four of the fifteen CHA members are large, multi-purpose (both service-providing and fund-raising) associations with budgets in excess of US$1 million (Alzheimer's; Leukaemia; Muscular Dystrophy; Multiple Sclerosis) and two others are major fundraisers (Juvenile Diabetes and Cystic Fibrosis). The policy is aimed less at them than at the other, mostly very small, multi-purpose associations with tiny chapter offices. Whether they concur and willingly take steps towards pooling resources remains to be seen, but the omens are far from encouraging. The deep-seatedness of the culture of autonomy or 'turfism' has been identified as a major feature of their culture: the executive director earlier cited as having been instructed on appointment to work to a policy of competition is from this group of CHA members. Significantly, in interviews for this study, the chapter executive directors made no mention of even the existence of CHA unless prompted, despite their compulsory monthly attendance at its meetings. Overcoming such entrenched attitudes is likely to be problematic, unless CHA has something more to offer. Aware of this, CHA's executive director was actively seeking premises large enough to house several chapters and other facilities for activities, as an inducement to joint working.

CONCLUSIONS

Office-based chapters are well established in St Louis. They range from the large service-provider United Cerebral Palsy Association, looking physically more like an outpatient or community care facility than a charity, to several very small (one or two staff) offices. Functionally, some chapters focus on fund-raising to finance research, some on providing support services, and some are multi-purpose, doing both. Only a small minority are consciously political, regularly lobbying health policy makers.

The office gives an association the appearance of strength. It symbolizes established activity and authoritative existence. In practical terms, it is a base and a fixed address. It often stimulates volunteer activity, with large numbers of unpaid helpers in several offices. Even the most basic of modern technology – a telephone, photocopier, computer, fax machine – makes an office a communications headquarters in a way that being based in someone's home does not. In America this actually means benefiting from free postage of all association circulars and newsletters, a not insignificant financial perk of charitable status which induces extensive mailing lists and enables associations to circulate health providers and professionals as well as members and supporters. (Local telephone calls are also free in St Louis, but that applies equally to home-based chapters). Not all chapters manage to operate very effectively: variable performance characterizes the chapters of patients' associations.

Some associations were achieving little, despite having loyal and energetic staff. The evidence above of support services, training and education activity, and fund-raising outcomes was patchy, with clear signs of underachievement in all three categories. In short, working out of an office is no sure guarantee of success. Whether underperformance reflects the modest levels of some salaries (which in turn limits the talent available, even though charitable work attracts many good people willing to work at such levels of pay) or the consequence of small-scale on the cost-effectiveness of an organization because staff become 'jack of all trades but master of none' is unclear, and a combination of these two factors probably applies. What is clear, however, is that the potential advantages of offices and paid staff are not necessarily fully realized in practice.

Variability also applies to the political activities of the chapters studied. Some campaigned quite actively on cost, access and consumer issues, and it was noted in Chapter 6 that one chapter (Alzheimer's Association) had appointed a dedicated public policy coordinator, jointly with the four other Alzheimer's chapters in Missouri. Others explained their almost total inaction on the conditions of charity status. At all points on this spectrum, coalition activity was notable by its absence, and the Missouri Consumer Health Care Watch was, despite its title, virtually bereft of health members.

It is hard to conclude other than that turfism, coupled with the belief that competition is just as commendable and healthy in the charity field as it is in industry and commerce, appeared to be the basis of American philanthropic culture and valued above all other characteristics, with consequences for chapter performance. Examples of cooperation, collaboration or coalition activity were so rare as to be exceptional (interestingly, many executive directors initially claimed that American politics is coalition politics and that a plethora of coalitions was at work in the health and welfare fields, but they were unable to offer any local examples as evidence in support of this belief).

Interviewees could always find reasons why working together

was unsatisfactory. For example, when asked why it was not possible to jointly train volunteers working at summer camps for youths
with particular health conditions (several associations provided
such camps as both a holiday experience for the campers and a
respite for their carers), executive directors responded unhesitat-
ingly that 'every camp is different' or that 'our campers have different needs'. Questions about swimming programmes, leisure and
social activities, and support group leadership invariably received
similar responses. That any training of volunteers might possibly
overlap and thus be duplicated was, it was made very clear, not a
matter for serious consideration.

In Britain the local branches of patients' associations are predominantly all-volunteer, home-based organizations. Seven St
Louis chapters, not covered above, operated on a similar basis.
How does this alternative model of local organization compare with
the St Louis office-based approach? A tentative evaluation is made
in Chapter 9, where the Manchester experience is first outlined.

9

GREATER MANCHESTER – LOCAL WEAKNESS?

Identifying the extent of patients' association local activity across the Greater Manchester conurbation ('Manchester') unexpectedly proved to be highly problematic. The geographical simplicity of its division into just ten large Metropolitan Boroughs, each coterminous with a single health authority (until NHS mergers in the mid-1990s reduced their number to only six), was more than offset by the difficulties of tracking down organizations which were volunteer-led, usually with an address which was a member's home, and which might well experience rotating officeholders, scattered memberships (frequently going beyond the conurbation's outer boundaries) and sometimes ephemeral existences. Cross-checks of separate lists maintained by borough council public libraries, by NHS authorities, and by Councils of Voluntary Service invariably raised inconsistencies, if only because each body began any periodic updating from its existing database, and there was no indication of attempts to develop a common approach.

Eventually, 82 of the 225 national associations originally listed and analysed in Chapters 3 and 4 were identified as having, or, rather, as claiming to have, some form of regional or local organizational activity in Manchester. At first sight this is 29 more than the 53 initially identified in Chapter 8 as allegedly active St Louis, but the figures are neither truly comparable nor strong evidence of higher levels of British local activity.

Comparability is somewhat more robust if all cases of distant regional offices, of home-based individuals styled 'regional contacts' (not sought in St Louis), of closed-down branches, and of hospital clinic addresses are excluded. Within Manchester this left 61 associations with one or more branches, compared with 47 in

St Louis. In a few cases there were separate branches in each borough: the British Diabetic Association actually had 12 in the ten boroughs; the Multiple Sclerosis Society 9, for example, but these were the exceptions. In no fewer than 33 of the 61 cases there was just one single branch operating somewhere in the conurbation, while in ten further instances there were only two branches.

Data were collected for as many of the 61 associations claiming local activity as possible through a combination of postal survey, analysis of national newsletters and (mainly telephone) interviews. In comparison even to the considerable variation in activity found within St Louis in Chapter 8, the extent to which Manchester branches were truly active varied enormously, from *de facto* moribund to large, lively bodies.

In the 1997 national postal survey of British patients' associations many respondents attached great significance to their branches. Branches were variously described as 'a lifeline for women with endometriosis' (National Endometriosis Society, with over 40 groups nationwide but only one in Manchester and none in neighbouring Lancashire or Merseyside) and as 'the backbone of the Trust' (National Meningitis Trust, with 65 affiliated groups but again only one in the conurbation). Claims of a 'national network' of branches covering the country were commonplace even where associations had far smaller numbers than these. Local activity clearly symbolizes strength in the minds of senior management at national headquarters.

Behind this perhaps natural tendency to overstate the scale of branch coverage of the country, what did emerge was that a significant number of national associations listed branch development in their strategic plans as a high-priority objective and that in some cases considerable efforts and resources were being allocated to this issue. National Lottery funding for salaried local or regional development officer appointments had often been sought, inevitably with mixed success. A bid from the Toxoplasmosis Trust for Regional Coordinators was one that had failed, whereas the National Eczema Society, the Neurofibromatosis Association and the Crohn's in Childhood Research Association were three of at least eight associations which had obtained Lottery awards for this area of activity. The BBC Children in Need fund and Department of Health (DoH) grants had provided alternative sources of funding for branch development in other cases including the National Endometriosis Society (DoH, for a Support Network Manager) and STEPS: National Association for Children with Lower Limb

Abnormalities (BBC, for a review of regional development), while Coutts Bank had funded a three-year development officer post to stimulate new branches of the Hodgkin's Disease Association.

These and other initiatives such as the Leukaemia Care Society's decision in 1998 to use existing funds to appoint a full-time national volunteers' coordinator reflect growing concerns about the variable nature of all-volunteer branches and a realization of the need to improve support systems for those who do volunteer locally. Recruiting unpaid officers to ensure succession within a branch, or to establish new branches, has not been easy in the 1990s, and – as in America – associations are having to respond to the more crowded marketplace for volunteers. The Macular Disease Society, for example, reported that of its 46 branches nationally the one in Manchester had been particularly 'large and thriving' but was likely to close 'because the two organizers are unable to continue and no one has been found to take it on'. And the Prader–Willi Syndrome Society, in rather an understatement, was 'somewhat disappointed' that 'only one parent responded to our request (made nationwide in its newsletter) to start up a local group'.

As well as help with volunteer recruitment, the need to offer branch officials ongoing support, guidance and training was also being increasingly recognized. However, meeting this need remained particularly patchy, ranging from no more than statements of intent or wish lists to functional advisory documents, such as branch support packs and guidelines/handbooks, and to regular developmental training courses and seminars in the case of a handful of the larger associations, especially where there was a salaried staff presence either at a regional office or working from home.

The analysis of branch activity in Manchester follows a similar format to the previous chapter on St Louis. The broad backdrop has now begun to emerge: enormous variety between branches; many national associations embracing policies designed to increase local activity levels; and broad evidence that associations are right to have concerns about branch vitality and to act to enhance support systems to underpin local voluntary efforts.

STRUCTURE AND AUTONOMY

The Charities Act 1993 introduced statutory changes to the legal setting within which the branches of all types of national charity operated. National associations had no choice but to review the constitutional status of their branches, and this brought local activity to the top of many agendas. To simplify, branches needed either to register with the Charity Commissioners as a separate charity and thus work within a federal-type national association constitution, or to have their accounts (when the sums of money were more than trivial) externally audited or inspected and consolidated into the national accounts of a unitary parent association.

By the time of this study (1997–8) the vast majority of associations had adopted, or continued to utilize, the unitary model of branches as 'all part of one charity' (as Arthritis Care, with a massive 637 local branches and groups, described it). Thus British Liver Trust branches were 'responsible to BLT' under their 'agreements' with it. A second category was operating a twin-track system: in the case of Headway, with 112 affiliated local self-help groups (three in Manchester) and 40 Headway House day care centres (none in Manchester), 'more of our groups are becoming independently registered as charities, reflecting how their viability has improved'. Third, others had become entirely federal as with the Ileostomy and Internal Pouch Support Group: 52 of its 55 'autonomous' local groups in England and Wales (two in Manchester) had become separate charities with the other three too small to make registration worthwhile as their incomes were under £1000. Similarly, the Association for Spina Bifida and Hydrocephalus had seen each of its 64 branches, five of them in Manchester, become independent charities.

A fourth and final category of associations were in the midst of rethinking their structures. The National Schizophrenia Fellowship, for example, with over 200 branches and a regional office for the whole of northern England in central Manchester, was employing consultants to advise on the case for establishing regional charities.

Much less positively, the National Society for Phenylketonuria (with one of its ten branches in Manchester) viewed the outcome of the Charities Act changes in stark terms: 'local groups have been hit badly . . . the complexity of running a fully registered charity group is daunting', and the Stillbirth and Neo-natal Death Society had found that the legal changes had created 'extra work' for little or no benefit. Within the unitary category, subtle differences in the precise central/local relationship remained, with some branches able to exert more autonomy than others. For example, the National Back Pain Association (NBPA), described its 61 branches (only one in Manchester) as 'semi-autonomous'. NBPA branches had powers which included the ability to set their own levels of subscriptions.

This enforced review of branch structures had frequently generated controversy, causing internal divisions within associations. Annual reports showing apparently unified accounts often made minimal comment about tricky change processes, which is unsurprising given that they are broadly meant to convey good news to supporters and the public. However, some annual reports and survey responses did reveal enough tensions in the central/local relationship to indicate that unified accounts are far from an accurate indication that an association operates with one single pot of money gleaned and distributed harmoniously. There clearly had been instances of local antipathy about contributing towards what were locally perceived as quite large headquarters management costs (not always surprising given the evidence of spending on 'overheads' detailed in Chapter 5), and even sometimes about forwarding fund-raising income. Often this antipathy predated the recent legal changes but they caused it to emerge publicly.

A good example of the public admission of internal tensions was the Multiple Sclerosis Society (MSS), with nine of its 344 British branches in Manchester. In the 1996 annual report the MSS treasurer noted that branch contributions to central funds had not changed in the five years 1991–6, remaining at about £1 million a year (an average of around £2700 each). Their 'seeming reluctance to contribute adequately . . . will need to be addressed' he declared. Elsewhere in the same annual report the chairman was more diplomatic, recognizing that branch 'autonomy' had been a matter of 'pride', though also indicating that 'we now need to work more closely together . . . to reflect the changing times we live in. We need our branches more than ever'. He went on to suggest that 'common policies' were also a necessity. These tensions continued. A commissioned Brunel University review of MSS's regional support systems led to a proposed package of changes. At the 1997 annual meeting these were challenged: a motion was tabled for 'reference back' on the grounds that branches had been given inadequate time to discuss them.

Lupus UK, with 26 regional self-help groups (that in Manchester boasted Sir James Anderton, former controversial chief constable, as its patron) and with local branches within each of them, was also facing controversy. The 1997 chair's report proposed that the association 'integrate local group balances into the overall accounting procedure' as it moved towards developing a 'single entity charity', though it was recognized that this 'may be a thorny issue with some'. The chair's aims included developing training for branch officials, not least because the branch was seen as having an important political role to play through 'helping raise local awareness'.

BRANCH SIZE

Before reviewing the size, activities and functions of branches in Manchester it is first necessary to unpick the generic term 'branch'. Linguistic differences between associations – some use the title branch, others group, association, club, and so on – have no significance for this study. Organizational and functional variations, however, can have consequences both for the central/local relationship within an association and for the potential ability of branches to act politically to influence health care (their political role was noted in Chapter 6 as limited: this initial conclusion will be developed and confirmed in the section 'Liaison and collaboration' below).

Four types of local organizational arrangement were identified in Manchester. First, there were some associations which had named individual local 'contacts' in the area but no obvious signs of any collective activity which could properly be labelled a branch (nor did they use such a term). One example is the Tracheo-oesophagal Fistula Society, nationally an all-volunteer association, with one of its 'local coordinator contacts' in the conurbation. No meetings could be identified, and the support activity appeared to be entirely on a one-to-one basis with families. In other cases the equivalent person occasionally did arrange meetings. Thus the 'regional contact, families network' local representative of the Myotonic Dystrophy Support Group convened one about every six months; one or two meetings each year were arranged in the north west by the 'contact' of the Primary Immunodeficiency Association; and the British Colostomy Association held occasional open days rather than 'regular self-help group meetings', although its area organizer was also responsible for recruiting volunteers. As these and other similar instances do not constitute meaningful, ongoing local collective activity they have not been defined as constituting a branch or included in the analysis which follows.

A second distinction relates to the definition of a branch as a geographical entity. Groupings (sometimes labelled as 'branches') based on categories of members, and therefore on non-spatial or wider regional arrangements, were identified. Often such groups operated alongside the geographical branches of this study. Arthritis Care was one of several associations to have separate groups for young people with arthritis – it had 610 branches organized geographically and covering fairly small communities such as a single Manchester borough, and 27 Young Arthritis Care groups loosely based on much larger areas (and hence excluded hereafter).

Third, some branches were more formally constituted than others and this was sometimes recognized in association constitutions. The British Polio Fellowship (BPF), for example, defined a branch as 'properly constituted, with a committee, financial systems', whereas its 'groups' had neither of these basic components. In Manchester the BPF had just one group and no branch, and the group had the appearance of being an individual energetic activist operating largely alone to raise both funds and public awareness. Quite similarly, the National Endometriosis Society (NES) separated its 40 groups, each being an 'elected committee, all NES members, properly accountable to the Society's Trustees' from its seven clubs which lacked committees and bank accounts. This study encompasses both formal and informal local organizations, provided they had ongoing collective activity.

Finally, branches might be single- or multi-purpose organizations. The former were usually either support or self-help groups only, or fund-raisers only. The British Heart Foundation, for example, had 437 'voluntary fund-raising branches' across Britain (10 in Manchester) but claimed also that it had 'helped set up 193 support groups' which operated quite separately. Three mental illness associations – Depression Alliance, the Manic Depression Fellowship and the Fellowship of Depressives Anonymous – each ran single-purpose self-help groups 'to support and encourage each other' (Fellowship of Depressives Anonymous) or for 'a safe, supportive space . . . to express their experiences and exchange support and information' (Manic Depression Fellowship), with eight between them in Manchester.

Much more common, however, were multi-purpose branches. Sometimes that was not immediately obvious from association constitutions. The Coeliac Society had 54 branches (one in Manchester) whose role was to 'provide self-help locally' under the Society's aims, but they were described rather differently in the national newsletter (*The Crossed Grain*) as offering 'social, fund-raising and informative activities'. Where multi-purpose branches did exist, they did not necessarily provide the full range of activities, as their strength varied: the 39 branches of the Dystonia Society (one in Manchester) included 'some on a purely social basis, others are expert fund-raisers'.

The 61 associations with Manchester branches held their open meetings in a variety of settings: clinics, church halls, libraries, even public houses. Committee meetings were usually at members' homes because the typical branch committee was only about six strong: chair, secretary, treasurer and two or three other members. The contrast here with the St Louis chapter boards reviewed in Chapter 8 is particularly clear-cut, not just in terms of size (20–30 directors against six members) but also in that the Manchester committees comprise solely activist members who commonly are carers or people with the condition. There is almost no attempt to co-opt prominent names from the business, sporting or social community onto committees in order to raise the branch's profile – indeed, the earlier reference to a former chief constable as patron was itself highly unusual, and many association constitutions deliberately limit branch committees to members only.

Some branches have fairly large memberships of up to one hundred, but a dozen or two is more common. Founded only in April 1996, eighteen months later the (only) Manchester group of the Hodgkin's Disease Association reported over ninety members. The Bury branch of the Multiple Sclerosis Society (one of nine in Manchester) alone had 93 members in 1997. More typical is the British Epilepsy Association (BEA). It reported that its 146 branches across Britain 'involve regularly an estimated 4000 volunteers', or an average of 25 each. The four Manchester branches include one in Salford formed only in July 1997. BEA experience was, as with other associations, one of some instability: headquarters was reluctant to furnish names for interviews mainly because 'people come and go and any list . . . would quite soon become out of date'.

These concerns about transient branches and officials were echoed: the Bolton group of the Neurofibromatosis Association had failed and a meeting 'to try to get it going again' was being called. This process was made easier because a National Lottery award was funding a national network coordinator specifically to expand branch activity. REACH: the Association for Children with Hand or Arm Deficiency listed branch development as one of its four 'key areas we need to concentrate on' following an organizational review. Its newsletter ('Within Reach') reported that 'a number of branches really struggle to get members along which is very soul-destroying for the hard-working coordinator'. The Progressive SupraNuclear Palsy Association described its groups as 'loosely knit', offering as an explanation that 'the carer has no time to attend local group meetings': its sole branch in the whole of the north west has 32 members. All these examples come from associations representing long-term medical conditions. Perhaps less surprising was that associations representing acute medical conditions find it particularly hard to sustain active branches. The National Association for Premenstrual Syndrome is typical: its branches 'tend to fade away as the participants learn to cope with, or overcome, their PMS difficulties'.

As in St Louis, there is a strong Manchester link in the geography of branches between poverty, social class and branch strength. The discussion in Chapter 7 of an inverse relationship between needs and supply is confirmed. The largest branches are in the more affluent suburban boroughs, and 31 of the 33 associations with just one Manchester branch gave suburban contact addresses for it (in three cases the contact officer actually lived outside the conurbation).

Explicit concerns about inactivity levels and the difficulty of encouraging participation in the inner city were sometimes expressed. The Sickle Cell Society in its 1995–6 annual report noted 'a significant slump in the number of "active" support groups'. Although in crisis nationally at the time (see Chapter 7), its Manchester group was seen as fortunate in having a nationally known and very active centre manager to ensure that it continued. Nationally very much stronger, with 288 branches in 1996–7 (an increase of 28 in one year) the Alzheimer's Disease Society nevertheless reported that 'large areas of the country, most notably in the big conurbations, still lack our presence'. A particularly graphic and moving account of the problem was offered by the National Back Pain Association (NBPA). Its branch development officer observed that although, with 61 branches of NBPA, numbers had reached their 'highest yet', the list no longer included the City of Manchester – the branch there had folded. His experience, doubtless one shared by colleagues in other associations, was that founding branches was 'easier in the suburbs and small towns'. In large cities branches 'are very difficult to raise . . . why can I not reach into the poorer inner cities with large ethnic populations and get anywhere near a successful branch?'

Most Manchester branches, then, are modest in size, volunteer-led, lacking in office facilities, run by very small committees and based in members' homes. They contrast sharply with the business model on which St Louis office-based chapters are constructed. Their financial scale, apart from those focusing largely on fundraising to support research, is equally modest. For example, an average turnover of only £1200 in 1996 was reported for the 114

British Epilepsy Association branches included in the national accounts. The 139 National Asthma Campaign branches forwarded just £276,000 to headquarters in 1996–7, a drop of £31,000, and less than £2000 each. The one Manchester branch of STEPS: National Association for Children with Lower Limb Abnormalities had 1996–7 accounts showing an income of only £1549 yet STEPS views the 21 branches as its 'lifeblood'. Many had lower figures than these, and few had higher ones. Instances of a £5000 annual turnover were quite exceptional.

SERVICES AND ACTIVITIES

As in St Louis, supportive activities and fund-raising tend to dominate the agendas of Manchester branches. But in Manchester there was less evidence than even the little found in St Louis of activity involving the deployment of political resources through offering professional education or campaigning to increase public awareness. As was noted in Chapter 6, the micro-level and intermediate-level political impact of both the St Louis chapters and the Manchester branches was extremely limited, with just a handful of exceptions, almost all of them in St Louis where they were led by chapters' salaried professional staff.

Supportive activities

Supportive activities in Manchester did not include any provision of branch helplines. As was noted in Chapter 4, there are plenty of such telephone advice systems run by patients' associations in Britain, but they all operate on a national basis. Support groups in Manchester are mostly branch-run and are usually the main activity of that branch, whereas the bigger St Louis chapters organize them as outreach activities. Thus in St Louis there is a single chapter office of the American Diabetes Association facilitating several support groups across the conurbation, whereas in Manchester the twelve branches of the British Diabetic Association are each a support group.

More than in America, emphasis in Britain is placed on informal one-to-one 'contacts' as a support system. Many associations provide members and people newly aware of a diagnosis with lists of such names, giving the home addresses and telephone numbers of the contacts. SERENE (formerly Cry-sis Support Group – for parents with 'crying, sleepless or demanding babies') has no branches but offers interaction with 'volunteers' in the area; the Cleft Lip and Palate Association lists 64 named 'area contacts' nationally, but has only 43 branches; the Fragile X Society has 21 'link members'; Marfan's Association has 59 'support networkers' including two in suburban Manchester; and the Interstitial Cystitis Support Group lists 33 'local coordinators'. A typical description of this type of supportive activity was offered by the Tuberous Sclerosis Association: its 30 'regional representatives' are 'a network of members with personal experience of TS who offer local support'. It is important to recall that in every case, and in other similar ones not listed here, these support contacts are all volunteers.

Support through branch meetings is of two kinds, and most branches use both. Some meetings are entirely informal exchanges of experiences and social events; on other occasions a visiting speaker (usually a doctor, nurse, therapist or other health professional) outlines new treatments and good practice. Meetings vary in frequency. The Manchester regional branch of the Urostomy Association holds only two or three a year with a speaker. A stoma nurse attends them to offer advice, and appliance companies give demonstrations and display their products. The twelve British Diabetic Association branches (for 'care, support and companionship') all meet in local hospitals, mostly bimonthly with variations either side depending on the enthusiasm of branch officials, again with regular voluntary inputs from appropriate health professionals. In some contrast, the lively and active Cheetham Hill Support Group of Lupus UK meets monthly with an average attendance of 25: a specialist nurse from a local hospital attends voluntarily.

As these examples show, the regular unpaid support and assistance received from NHS professional staff is a frequent feature of the British branch scene, both in Manchester and elsewhere. That this is much more marked in Manchester than in St Louis in part reflects the ethos of Britain's National Health Service as a community entitlement. NHS hospitals and clinics are perceived as publicly owned open-access facilities, and the culture of the health 'caring professions' embraces this notion of voluntary outreach or extracurricular activities.

Professional education and training

Branch level activity in the area of professional education and training is almost non-existent. Manchester branches are all-volunteer bodies and their officials are in essence patients and carers, perceiving themselves as the recipients of health services first and foremost, and not as the shapers of those services. As 'lay' people they have no vision of developing a training relationship with the professionals on whom they depended. Rather, they are always grateful when health professionals are willing to speak at their meetings, and they seek to behave supportively so as to develop good relations with local hospitals and clinics. In essence, branches and their members play the role of passive partners in an unequal power relationship between providers and consumers.

There are exceptions, most clearly at the regional officer level which lay outwith this study. For example, the (salaried) regional director of the Manic Depression Fellowship, accompanied by a volunteer member of one of its self-help groups, addresses social worker training courses at Lancaster University twice a year. Other salaried officials in the region, including those of the British Diabetic Association and the Sickle Cell Society, also contribute to professionals' continuing education programmes.

At the all-volunteer branch level, however, only two possible instances of participation in professional education were identified. The branch chair of the Vitiligo Society manned an information stall about the society and its members' needs at the British Association of Dermatologists (the relevant professional body) throughout its 1997 annual meeting in Harrogate, seeking to enhance professionals' awareness of patients' needs. And the two local coordinators of the Toxoplasmosis Trust had given presentations to both a hospital maternity unit and local schoolteachers. In this case it was probably no coincidence that they themselves were a midwife and a paediatric nurse. In short, branch involvement by lay volunteers in professional education and training in Manchester is minimal and is not viewed as a normal branch role.

Fund-raising

Fund-raising activity, on the other hand, is commonplace. Here there is in one important respect a sharp contrast with experience in St Louis. In the Manchester branches, virtually all the fund-raising activities are aimed at members, supporters and the general public. The business community, charitable foundations, sporting and media celebrities, and corporate donors tend not to be the focus of attention. Approaching them is seen to be the responsibility of the national officers, salaried or not, at headquarters or in regional offices. Consequently, branch fund-raising is ongoing, frequent and energetic, but is extremely small-scale in nature. Branches themselves cost little to run, and most of the money raised is divided between donations to local hospitals for equipment or patient facilities and contributions to headquarters. Branch contributions to national accounts were earlier noted as generally low, and there are two reasons for this. First, local causes often have more appeal to members, and, second, because the whole branch fund-raising exercise is so limited.

Perhaps the most dramatic illustration of the Anglo-American contrast is offered by the Juvenile Diabetes Foundation (JDF). It was noted in Chapter 8 that the St Louis chapter of JDF alone raised US$476,000 (about £300,000) in 1996–7. That same year the JDF's total income from all local fund-raising activities across the whole of Britain was only £27,269. Over £10,000 of that came from a single effort, a sponsored walk in Liverpool. This study did not uncover any other event of that magnitude run by branch-level volunteers, in Manchester or elsewhere.

Much more typical are the experiences of the Manchester branch of the British Sjogren's Syndrome Association, which raised £58 in a raffle at a meeting with an expert speaker and a 'fantastic' £510 through its big event, the annual raffle with over eighty donated prizes. Many examples of far smaller amounts than these were reported in the survey of branch activity. Among the more successful branch fund-raisers in Manchester are Lupus UK, where an 'Irish night' netted £2000, a dinner dance £1700, and a folk night £500, all during spring 1997; the National Association for Colitis and Crohn's Disease, South Manchester branch, which raised £1800 from a 'swimathon' in April 1997, £900 from a garden party in June and £2000 from a champagne raffle over the summer; meanwhile its Wigan, Leigh and District branch handed over £5000 in June 1997 towards the purchase of an enteroscope for use by NHS staff. Another branch to support the NHS is the Manchester group of the Hodgkin's Disease Association which attracted over 200 people to its charity ceilidh and barn dance in February 1997, raising £625 each for its own funds and for a Christie (cancer) Hospital Appeal.

Overall, both the inventive range of initiatives and the large numbers of events indicate high levels of energy and enthusiasm amongst volunteer fund-raisers in the Manchester branches. However, it is hard to avoid concluding that, judged collectively, these efforts often result in much lower returns than might be obtained if some additional professional advice and support were available to branches. Contrast the above figures with those for St Louis given in Chapter 8, where salaried fund-raising specialists locally have the time and expertise to organize major events and to target corporate donors and celebrity sponsors. It is this latter gap which is particularly noticeable in the Manchester branches. Even if, as seems likely, they remain all-volunteer in the foreseeable future, the scope to become more 'professional' in their fund-raising activity is enormous, and those national associations investing in branch support systems have a very good chance of recouping their financial outlay – a not unimportant factor because National Lottery and other grants and awards tend to be for fixed periods of up to three years, by which time projects are expected to become self-funding.

LIAISON AND COLLABORATION

Two aspects of interassociation activity discussed in Chapter 8 in the analysis of St Louis related to the culture of competitiveness and to the extent of collaborative action, including political coalitions. Manchester lacks both aspects.

The competitiveness and autonomy of St Louis associations, a significant feature discussed at some length in Chapter 8, was far less apparent amongst Manchester branches. Even where there was apparent competition, because two or more associations related to the same clinical condition, relationships were generally harmonious. Take mental illness as an example. Three competing associations had a presence in Manchester and separately arranged local self-help support groups: the Manic Depression Fellowship was the largest, with a regional office in the city centre and six self-help groups in the conurbation; Depression Alliance (nationally with a similar sized budget) had one self-help group; so did the nationally much smaller Fellowship of Depressives Anonymous. Although each association functioned independently, their national and local newsletters, literature and publicity materials did include considerable cross-listing of self-help group contact details. This contrasted with the common practice in St Louis of ignoring the existence of competitor chapters.

This cross-referencing reflected a general feature of branch officials' attitudes in Manchester, although that is very different from concluding that it was universal in practice. Two obstacles to genuine ongoing liaison were that only a very few branches had their own regular newsletters anyway, so lists of any description were rare, and that there was a great deal of ignorance of the over-all pattern of patients' association activities amongst volunteer offi-cials. Manchester is a large conurbation, with ten autonomous boroughs, so a lack of knowledge of activities across the whole area is understandable. Slightly more surprising was that some volunteer activists seemed unaware of the existence within their fairly immediate locality of competing or overlapping associations, even where the national newsletters published by their parent associ-ations did inform them of the existence of related national associ-ations.

In addition, there was no Manchester equivalent to either United Way or the Combined Health Appeal of St Louis to bring branches together for cooperative fund-raising purposes, or to discuss common organizational problems. Councils of Voluntary Service (CVSs), long established coordinators of voluntary bodies, were borough-based and those contacted had no policy of calling meet-ings of health-related groups. Nor had the statutory community health councils (which represent the interests of NHS patients generally in each borough). Finally, no evidence of any patients' association convening local interbranch meetings emerged from the survey.

There was, then, no sign of collaborative or coalition activity across the branches in this study. The national umbrella organiz-ations highlighted in Chapter 6, including the skin care and neuro-logical campaigns, the Genetic Interest Group, and the Long-term Medical Conditions Alliance, all operated solely at a national level, with no policy of regional collaborative arrangements. Given their tiny manpower resources, that is not surprising.

The membership of community health councils (CHCs) includes a proportion elected by local voluntary groups. Here would seem an obvious place for branches to gain access to the NHS policy making process. However, the lists maintained by the NHS regional office of groups eligible to participate in the election process fre-quently failed to include branches identified by this study. As with CVS activity, those lists seemed more comprehensive in their coverage of local welfare and disability groups, probably because such groups are more narrowly based geographically, usually aligned to borough boundaries (because that is how social services are organized), than are many of the branches analysed here. It was noted that 33 of the 61 patients' associations with Manchester branches had only one branch, with ten others having only two. So branch membership commonly crossed borough (and therefore

CHC) boundaries, branch officers came from more than one borough, and there was no clear spatial base of the branch because it had no office accommodation. One consequence of these features was that recognition for purposes of CHC membership or voting was unlikely, and was dependent on branches seeking to become listed. The failure of most of them to initiate action explains why very few disease-related patients' associations were represented on CHCs. It also reflects both the apolitical culture of branch activists and the absence of effective guidance and training on the part of national associations.

It became apparent that the radical reforms of the NHS which took place from the late 1980s in no way motivated Manchester branches to respond through collaborative activities or political coalitions. Neither the separation of purchaser health authorities from provider NHS Trusts and consequent introduction of contracts in a quasi-market, nor the Patient's Charter focus on rights and expectations stimulated new thinking and fresh activities within branches. Not even low-level campaigning followed, and there was no evidence of attempts by branches individually, let alone through collective activity, to exert sustained pressure on local NHS agencies about access or quality issues. Any political influence was more by chance than design. Several dozen political organizations, with political resources and clear interests in improving public services, opted for the role of passive spectators during the struggles for power within the NHS in the 1990s.

THE ST LOUIS ALL-VOLUNTEER CHAPTERS

In Chapter 8 the St Louis analysis focused entirely on the 40 office-based chapters there. Although those 40 reflected the American approach towards chapter organization, there were a further seven chapters operating on an all-volunteer basis, without either offices or paid staff. They, of course, are directly comparable with the Manchester branches.

Contact was made with six, and four were interviewed. The chapter of International Rett Syndrome Association claimed to offer support groups though none could be found amongst lists in local newspapers. The couple who ran the chapter had a child with the condition and clearly operated under great pressure: they were keen but not well organized and the promised literature never arrived. In some contrast, the other three all ran newsletters, two operated at least one support group; two maintained lists of 'sympathetic doctors'; one raised US$20,000 through several fundraising events; one paid to be listed in the Yellow Pages; and two had displays at health fairs and for use in talks in schools.

These three were at least as active as the liveliest Manchester branches, and probably more so. Their memberships range from 30 to 35 'active' (Tourette Syndrome Association, TSA) to almost 50 (National Sjogren's Syndrome Association, NSSA) and about 80 in the case of the Spina Bifida Association (SBA). SBA had an unmanned office for storage of equipment and for meetings. Primarily a support group, its monthly chapter newsletter, with a circulation list of 400, does periodically call for lobbying activity, usually on the advice of national headquarters and on national issues (such as the campaign on 'Agent Orange', thought to be a source of birth defects). TSA and NSSA both offered the conventional explanations of their 'non-political' stances, though the latter was actually working with the chair of its medical advisory board to get a specialist clinic established in a local hospital, offering volunteer staff as an incentive to that hospital's managers.

These all-volunteer chapters are the poor relations of the St Louis scene. Two of the four aim to grow and become office-based. One already uses the Combined Health Appeal (CHA) premises for its meetings and is a supporter of the CHA policy of promoting shared offices. That their activity levels are above those found in Manchester reflects the existence of the larger office-based chapters as a kind of role model of apparently business-like activity: regular newsletters and so on are 'normal' for chapters in America, but are not for UK branches.

CONCLUSIONS

The contrasts between the Manchester all-volunteer branches and the St Louis salaried and office-based chapters reviewed in Chapter 8 were striking, though largely predictable. The chapters looked like businesses in both their organizational arrangements and their potential ability to act across a range of headings: support (especially noteworthy in the case of support offered to volunteer workers), professional training, fund-raising, and raising public awareness. They also competed like businesses, with little love lost between competitors in the fight for market share. Volunteer-led branches in Manchester inevitably had lower levels of activity, however hard the

core of volunteers worked. Not only did they not resemble businesses (unlike the volunteer chapters in St Louis which utilized the
same business language of boards and medical advisory panels even
though only two of the four studied had adopted the format of
having some non-member directors), they also did not see the business sector as a potential part of their wider environment, as a major
target for fund-raising or as a possible contributor of other resources.
Manchester thus had no equivalents to the ALS (motor neurone disease) chapter, with donated office space within a factory, one of
several with heavily subsidized offices through business sponsorship.

As many associations were recognizing, branches and volunteers
needed support to fulfil their potential. Many in Manchester operated without effective advice, guidance or personal 'hands-on' support from their parent bodies. This ensured instability, and periodic
branch failures were inevitable. With tiny committees, a very few
members had to achieve a great deal if a multi-purpose branch was
to maintain momentum. As officers became 'burnt out' there was
often no system of succession in place, and no central machinery for
identifying branch needs. If the new support structures contem-
plated by many associations are implemented, this should change.
As those structures frequently depended on short-term external
funding, a drive to create new branches and to underpin and
strengthen existing ones appears likely to happen.

There is no single 'best way' of organizing disease-related
patients' associations locally so as to guarantee success. In Manchester, as in St Louis (though in different ways), the evidence
points to unfulfilled potential. Energy, enthusiasm and commitment exist in some abundance but these invaluable attributes are
commonly offset by rather sketchy 'management' of volunteer
'labour'. One association to recognize that the volunteer marketplace is altering and that this requires a response is Arthritis Care.
Its 49-page June 1997 *Into The Millennium* consultative document
included awareness of 'a reduction in volunteers to help elderly or
disabled people and an increase of volunteers in other fields such as
environmental, international aid, human rights, and animal rights
issues'. Hence 'volunteers are becoming more demanding and are
looking [for] interesting opportunities for personal and career
development or for personal fulfilment in retirement'. Much was
said about headquarters/branch relations and the need to
strengthen its grassroots of 640 branches and 7000 active volunteers
as part of its 'strategic direction'.

The core of most branches – officers and activists with (or carers closely linked to) the clinical condition represented – is at first sight little affected by many of these perceived changes in volunteering. However, dynamic branches need to reach beyond the immediate captive audience in order to realize their full potential. Supplementing their resources by recruiting other altruistic volunteers who have different domestic pressures is one method. But many associations and branches positively discourage such recruitment by imposing rules that committees are open only to members (thus charging a subscription as a perverse reward for volunteering). Here surely is one simple starting place for reform if branch development is a serious agenda item.

The limited nature of branch activity in Manchester suggests that the rethink about branch policy taking place in many associations in the late 1990s was timely. Seven key findings emerge. Four relate to branches and volunteers generally: (1) branches are often ephemeral, with a mere handful of enthusiastic volunteer activists; (2) in such a setting it is hard, without management support from above, to maintain momentum long-term; (3) most activities are necessarily small-scale in nature, despite high levels of commitment; but (4) volunteers do appear to get much emotional satisfaction from working to improve the lot of people with particular medical conditions. The remaining three findings include further indications, through the home-based nature of branches and evidence of gaps in the network, that (5) activity levels are class-related, with inner cities particularly poorly covered; (6) the American 'business model' for branches is not favoured in terms of both basic organization or of targeting support and income, yet it has much to offer; and (7) there is ambivalence towards behaving politically to influence health care, with a tendency to adopt the role of subservient 'grateful patients'.

PART IV

CONCLUSIONS

10

CONCLUSIONS – PATIENTS' ASSOCIATIONS, POLITICS, STATES AND DEMOCRACY

'NOW YOU SEE THEM, NOW YOU DON'T!'

The central chapters of this book have uncovered, through surveying close to 500 British and American patients' associations, a hugely variable patchwork of political activity. Successes have included the sheer human endeavour behind the formation of these 500 disease-related patients' associations in Britain and America, well over half of them founded as recently as the 1980s early 1990s, and the very impressive evidence of the provision by them of a host of valuable supportive services (some physical but many of them psychological in nature and with much evidence of inventiveness and innovation) for those who make contact as a result of being diagnosed with the medical condition which the association represents. Important as this activity is (and it is seen by most of them as their key role, alongside fund-raising to encourage greater research efforts), it was in fact not central to this particular study, which has sought to focus on the *political* economy and *political* effectiveness of patients' associations, rather than to evaluate in any detail their specific records of service provision to members and supporters.

One early finding needs immediately to be restated. Political scientists began in the 1970s and 1980s to be interested in the politics of health: the two key American academic journals, for example, commenced publication in 1976 (*Journal of Health Politics, Policy and Law*) and in 1982 (*Health Affairs*). It was not until 1989 that a specialist Politics of Health Group was established within the Political Studies professional association in Britain. Yet our initial literature search in Chapter 1 reported an 'almost total neglect of the politics of patients' in the main texts on both health studies and on pressure groups. Mark Peterson from Harvard was the first to observe that a 'citizenry more educated, attuned to politics' was beginning to permeate health politics (Peterson 1993: 789–90), a line pursued in Britain by Michael Moran, as one consequence of the rise of market systems in health care (Moran 1998), partly because modern technologies such as home computers have made it easier to bring groups into existence and to sustain them alongside rising expectations which patients now have. Yet the neglect remains striking.

As an example, the journal *Policy and Politics* published a special edition 'Mental health and social order' (Manning and Shaw 1999). Although the nine articles from leading academic researchers included pieces on America and Italy, and although several of them discussed the rise of consumer involvement as a major theme in mental health services and policy developments, in every case the discussion was restricted to the role and influence of patients as individuals rather than collectively. It was as if, to the authors, major representative and advocacy patients' associations – such as SANE and MIND in Britain – simply did not exist. Apparently ignored were the facts that the latter alone has an annual turnover in excess of £5 million and a history over 50 years of campaigning successfully for public policy to centre on improved care in the community (its competitor, SANE, has in recent years advocated, with some success in terms of government pronouncements, for a return to more secure hospital-based psychiatric beds in the wake of periodic incidents involving violence from schizophrenic patients being treated in the community). Further, MIND has over 220 local branches and the extent of MIND's status of 'public legitimacy' is evidenced by its membership in 1997–9 of the government's advisory committee reviewing mental health policy, law and services, by the ongoing government funding of part of its legal advocacy work on welfare rights, and by its selection in 1997 to distribute £1 million of grant funding on behalf of the Millennium Commission.

ASSOCIATIONS AS EMERGING 'CHALLENGERS'?

The political science focus of this study entailed the search for power and influence. Associations have been here viewed, despite their common claim to be non-political organizations, as a new species of pressure group, interested in bettering the lot of those they claim to represent. In terms of the categories of pressure group found in that literature introduced in Chapter 1, they initially appear to be clear-cut instances of 'cause groups'. However, in practice they emerged as being more than that in that their remit of seeking to represent people with medical conditions clearly gives them a specific 'interests' focus too. Thus they in practice become a third or 'hybrid' category of pressure group to add to the two conventionally utilized of 'cause' and of 'interest' or 'sectional' groups. Interestingly, of the standard pressure group texts widely used in Britain in the 1980s and 1990s only Alderman (1984: 31, 40–1) actually gives serious discussion to the potential existence of this additional 'hybrid' category. In the case of most disease-related patients' associations their 'hybridity' and their political nature are most clearly reflected in their legal basis. As (mostly) registered charities they legally require a package of documentary baggage which includes a formal constitution, and this, in turn, normally includes a list of the organization's purpose or stated objectives. There is often a certain 'sameness' about these as language and phraseology is naturally widely 'borrowed', both within Britain or America and sometimes cross-nationally too, when constitutions are initially drafted and adopted at general meetings. To give a single but fairly typical instance, the constitution of the Interstitial Cystitis Support Group in the UK (ICSGUK, an association founded in 1994 by 'two sisters who suffer from the disease') includes as its 'objects':

(i) the relief of sickness of persons suffering from IC;
(ii) the advancement of education amongst the general public and the medical profession into the causes and treatment of IC;
(iii) the promotion of research into the causes and treatment of IC on terms that the results of such research are published.

Typical also was ICSGUK's claim in response to the 1997 postal survey that it was a 'non-political' organization, again a standard and conventional (amongst respondents to this study's surveys) claim. In practice, this 'non-political' claim is actually quite clearly inconsistent with its stated objects above. In Chapter 2 we introduced and defined 'politics' as being 'the process by which society's beliefs and values are converted into public policies' (Peterson 1993: 401). ICSGUK's object (ii) in particular is designed to challenge not only the existing patterns of NHS *resource distribution* in health care and research, but also *the belief systems of society* in general and those of health policy makers in particular. This is significant because the normal interpretation by associations of the phrase 'bettering the lot' of members, goes beyond the provision of services offering them private support to include activities aimed at raising the public profile of the disease through the search for a cure or for more effective treatment systems. Such activities might include campaigning for the provision of more specialist facilities, centres or clinics.

Our survey of Britain and America has thus clearly established that, whatever their claims to the contrary, patients' associations are self-evidently *political organizations*, existing in very large numbers and seeking to influence society's attitudes towards particular illnesses and diseases and in consequence to influence the distribution of resources for health care and medical research. They operate in what has been in both countries a fast-moving political environment of health care reform, which in itself raises further issues about their institutional framework.

Before we consider that, we first go back to the very beginning of this study. In the opening paragraph of the preface, reference was made to the pathbreaking study of health politics and of the various structural interests within it which Robert Alford undertook almost thirty years ago, and to the labels which he attached to the three key groups of 'structural interests' which he identified in the politics of New York's hospital system. His framework was developed further in Chapter 1 when the conventional academic view emerged of patients as largely passive and unimportant consumers of whatever the medical profession provided. Alford's depiction of political struggles as being primarily between the 'dominant' doctors and the 'challengers' from managerial actors seeking to implement corporate rationalization of health care was influential, particularly among British analysts. This influence was retained over time not least because the 1980s politics of health in Britain seemed to match almost precisely that analysis. The Thatcher governments appeared to mount a serious challenge to medical power through the introduction of much stronger management systems: in particular the introduction of general managers to head hospitals and provider units and health authorities after 1983, a system extended to the general practitioner services in 1989. Although the debate about medical power is far from over in Britain, most health texts have portrayed the period from the early 1980s as an era of rising managerial power and declining professional autonomy for the medical profession. One of the 1990s most widely used medical sociology texts, for example, opens with a section bluntly headed 'The rise of managerialism' in its first chapter which, significantly, is entitled 'From tribalism to corporatism: the managerial challenge to medical dominance' (Hunter 1994: 2).

Subscribers to the theory of managerial power might do worse than read the epilogue to that same text. Subtitled 'The last days of Doctor Power', and written in the style of a short play, it ends with an amusing and an unexpected twist designed to make the reader rethink that title.

If the power struggle between the dominant and the challengers is now largely resolved in the British NHS, then presumably this study might have accumulated some evidence that this new set of interests studied here could soon become conventionally viewed as the 'new challengers' to the now 'dominant' managerial interests? At first sight some of the health reforms of the 1990s might seem to offer some support for viewing disease-related patients' associations as the new challengers. In the UK the Thatcher/Major quasi-market reforms of the period 1990–7 certainly appeared to place heavy emphasis on the role and status of patients as consumers, both through the rhetoric of choice (of GP; of location of referral to a specialist) and through the consumer rights policies beginning with the Citizen's Charter but with the Patient's Charter tariff of entitlements soon following and with the publication of performance indicators in most mainstream public services, including health care. At least in this respect the Labour government after May 1997 sang to a remarkably similar tune, increasing the pressure on the NHS to cut its legendary and lengthy hospital waiting lists and in 1999 receiving proposals from the Dyke Committee which had reviewed the Patient's Charter and recommended further strengthening it in the interests of the patient as consumer. The earlier jargon of 'patients' voices' (NHS Management Executive 1992; see also Lewthwaite and Haffenden 1997) remained firmly embedded in the mind-set of policy makers.

However, it would be both misleading and unduly optimistic to pretend that there has been strong evidence in earlier chapters here that patients' associations in either Britain or America really look like embryonic 'new challengers' to the established interests of doctors, health professionals and, above all, of mainstream health providers and their senior managers. In particular, the insular mind-set which was found to dominate the world of patients' associations makes it hard to envisage effective ongoing political alliances or coalition activity and campaigns to alter the mind-sets of policy makers. At several points, most clearly in Chapter 6 in the section 'collaborative politics', the deep-seated attitude of autonomy which was found in the surveys was revealed. Furthermore that section went on to conclude (p. 109) that 'the overall picture is one of failure to work together to increase their ability to influence policy makers in both countries'. This was a study of the failure of associations to mobilize the considerable quantity of latent political resources which they either possess almost naturally or have chosen not to effectively acquire and mobilize. In 1997–8, the year of this survey, they certainly showed very few signs of being either interested in or capable of altering their behavioural characteristics towards transformation into anything even remotely resembling the label 'new challengers'. Yet they frequently do share common ambitions. In particular, many associations seek improved specialized facilities for the treatment of certain conditions (the Stroke Association in Britain being one of many examples). Other common causes include demands for speedier access to the latest drugs, and for higher levels of public spending on medical research. In short, there is the potential for coalition activity but it has so far led to little in the way of alliance-building.

INSTITUTIONAL ISSUES

Patients' associations, creatures of the last three decades of the twentieth century, collectively constitute 'big business' as multibillion dollar (or pound) charities with large memberships and considerable numbers of paid employees. Indeed there has emerged in parallel with the rapid rising numbers of charities in both countries what amounts to a new profession, that of 'charity management'. In the case of Britain this was further underpinned at the end of the century by the introduction of the National Lottery which proceeded to distribute large sums of money to many voluntary organizations, while simultaneously creating problems for the nonrecipients who found that charity-giving by the general public dipped.

The 1990s also saw the further emergence of what is commonly termed 'the contract state', increasingly using what became styled as 'the third sector' of voluntary, non-profit and other non-governmental organizations to implement public policy through a process of 'bidding' for funds, usually for a limited amount of time. Thus several British associations had successfully bid for NHS funds and in a sense had moved partly into being providers of NHS services rather than purely advocacy organizations. They were in a sense 'instruments of government' and this affected their management style, not least in terms of the role of the unpaid board members at their head (Harris 1998). The questionnaire survey to British patients' associations received contrasting responses to its enquiry about the impact of the new (from 1990) NHS contract state. SCOPE reported this as having had a 'profound effect' on its organization. The Royal Association in Aid of Deaf People had had 'to adapt senior management to meet fresh challenges from the contract culture'. In complete contrast Foresight, the association for the promotion of pre-conceptual care ('to secure the health of parents' with foci on infertility and nutrition and leaflets and a video to educate prospective parents along with a 234-page book on the subject), reported of the introduction of the quasi-market in 1990: 'I am not aware [of] . . . any effect on our work' (probably because it was an all-volunteer organization with no apparent contracts in place or sought).

As the century ended, reports of difficulties in attracting funds, whether by traditional donation or by the new bidding system, arose sufficiently frequently that the leading British studies of voluntary bodies (Kendall and Knapp 1996; Philpot and Hanvey 1996) devoted space to a discussion of how these bodies could continue to survive, given that many lacked the 'natural' membership of patients' associations who hope to recruit from people diagnosed with certain specific conditions, in many cases with a clear idea of how many potential recruits there might be due to epidemiological data on the incidence of the disease or condition. The major study – Kendall and Knapp – focused empirically on education and law and not on the health sector.

The focus here has not been on either legal or institutional arrangements, but on the actual activities of associations. But the usual political issues do arise in patients' associations. One such is accountability, particularly where the larger associations like SCOPE seek simultaneously both to provide services and to campaign politically. Through contracts they act in partnership with, and in effect almost as part of the state, the very body which they want to actively criticize and campaign against. White (1999) is an example of this concern, arguing that the service-providing and campaigning activities shoud be strictly separated in the regulations surrounding the legal status of a charity. The service/campaigning distinction applies most clearly in mental health and in HIV/AIDS charities within the ambit of this survey. In Britain it also applies to lobbying on behalf of 'carers' which was beyond the scope of this study because it does not relate to a specific clinical condition.

A second area which arose earlier is the central/local relationship within health charities: in short this centres on the extent of power which local branches or chapters have over activities, spending decisions and the like. Too much central control is potentially frustrating and can stifle local initiative, and several associations had to review their constitutions in the late 1990s. In earlier chapters, examples of different constitutional models arose in both Britain and America. In the former, 1990s charities rule changes brought up the issue in terms of new rules about separate branch status if more than a fairly small amount of money is involved. There are no clear criteria for what qualifies for recognition as a charity and in both countries qualifiers include bodies which do not immediately strike one as likely charities (private fee-paying schools in Britain and the giants of American football, the Denver Broncos, are often cited as fortunate to obtain the tax-breaks which registered charities receive). There is clearly room for more work to be done on these rules, perhaps to develop simpler criteria which charities should have to meet to obtain formal recognition. (One leading charity chief executive has suggested three criteria, which the vast majority of the disease-related patients' associations studied here meet either in their constitutions or through their main activities: (1) most income from voluntary efforts and donations; (2) stated aims to include campaigning and awareness-raising; (3) user empowerment (Gutch 1999).)

What was striking was the very varied rate and extent of local or branch development in both the case study areas of Manchester and St Louis, as well as the totally contrasting models favoured (business model in America; all-volunteer home-based in Manchester). Given the pressures under which contemporary charities operate, it was perhaps heartening to note the extensive evidence that many associations are pursuing policies of strengthening their local presence, either through encouraging the growth of new branches or chapters, or through providing much better basic support for local volunteers through developing more organized middle-management through improved intermediate or regional-level officers and offices, particularly in Britain. There is no doubt that the relatively unstable British branches could benefit greatly from this and it will be interesting to see how successful those associations pursuing this policy prove to be in the coming decade, at a time when recruitment of volunteers is seemingly becoming more difficult as people face more and more alternative ways of spending their spare time.

PATIENTS' ASSOCIATIONS AND THE STATE

In both Britain and America the attitude of the state towards patients' associations has always been and remains critical to their chances of being politically effective. This is most obvious in Britain, because of the government-run National Health Service. Funded out of general taxation and giving all citizens access to free care when they need it, the NHS was installed in 1948 through absorbing into the apparatus of the state hundreds of hospitals previously provided by the voluntary charitable sector, which had been 'the dominant mode for the formal delivery of social welfare up until the early 20th century' (Kendall and Knapp 1996: 248). Hence the state/charity relationship in Britain has been one of mutual interdependence, with the latter moving later from being senior to junior partner. Although in America at first sight the majority of health care spending is through private insurance, the state is in practice almost as important to patients' associations as is the case in Britain. This is for three reasons. First, the American federal government is a major funder, through the National Institutes of Health, of research. Second, the federal government is a major provider of health care to the poor, disabled and elderly (who collectively are particularly prone to the conditions many of the associations studied earlier represent). And third, the state, both at the federal and at the state level, is also heavily involved in the regulation of many aspects of 'private' health care, from controls over the new managed care organizations to the licensing of health technologies and of hospitals, large numbers of which began as philanthropic institutions. American patients' associations may also legitimately target insurance companies, doctors and employers too about issues of access, cost or quality, but they are almost always likely to see the political system as an important route to improved funding, enhanced access to care, and to the availability of new treatment regimes.

The state's attitude towards patients' associations (and other philanthropic voluntary organizations not examined in this study) can often be interpreted as ambivalent. The charity movement offers at one level a 'quality add-on supplement' to mainstream health provision. It provides the extras which are either not afford-able as mainstream provision or not readily available (for example, advice from fellow patients and a host of broadly similar contact and mentoring schemes styled variously as anything from penpals to buddy schemes, designed to provide not just support but reassur-ance and confidence). There is, at least in theory, a very clear dis-tinction between this activity and one possible contrasting state approach of seeking to utilize charities to 'plug basic holes' in public services. However, in practice this boundary is blurred, sometimes because innovative health charities may introduce an experimental service development which, because of its success, becomes accepted as mainstream service provision (when this happens it illustrates enormous political influence).

In this study some evidence did emerge of associations which were providing manpower and funds to underpin the basic opera-tions of some clinics, laboratories, and medical and nursing teams (see Chapter 5, pp. 85–6). In short, the contemporary state con-tinues to have some record of quite unashamedly using associations as cheap mainstream providers and as the central and leading fun-ders of basic research. In Britain this record is beginning to extend to the deployment of monies raised by the National Lottery, despite initial assurances that its funds would not be utilized to provide basic services. In March 1999, for example, a plan was announced to use £200 million of Lottery monies to improve access to cancer services despite this being a policy published earlier in a White Paper as part of the Labour government's reform of the NHS.

Positive attitudes amongst the general public towards charities of all kinds means that substantial numbers of people are willing to work voluntarily on an unpaid basis and to donate often substantial sums of money to patients' associations. In Britain most of the sums invested in cancer research are still provided by health charities: the NHS may be responsible for treating cancer cases (despite its recourse to Lottery proceeds) but its input into basic research to overcome the disease remains extremely limited. In this and other instances of financing medical research the state lives somewhat parasitically off the goodwill of the public, in a manner reminiscent of the pre-welfare state era. In both countries, but particularly in America, the culture and attitudes of the business and commercial sectors include the notion of corporate social responsibility and the sponsorship by them of fund-raising events is particularly marked (though noted in Chapter 9 as being largely absent at the local level

of associational activity in Britain). The British and American welfare states may have resulted in changes to the role of charities, no
longer basic providers of health care on a large scale, but the legacy
remains and states receive significant financial and manpower support from patients' associations. American 'not-for-profit' hospitals
with religious foundations perhaps remain as a last vestige of the
pre-welfare state health care system, but today they are funded
largely by the state and by employers' insurance schemes, are not
easily distinguishable from the 'for-profits' in organizational and
managerial terms, and are by no means the sole locations of the
provision of indigent care.

For some patients' associations studied here the key relationship
with the state has centred on the basic campaign for disease recognition which lay behind their original foundation, and their successes again reflect enormous political influence. For the state, the
implications go well beyond the provision of health care: the even-
tual acceptance in both countries of, for example, chronic fatigue
syndrome, repetitive strain injury or, in Britain in January 1999,
vibration white finger (prevalent amongst coalminers) has a far
greater financial impact on social security entitlements to pensions
and disability benefits than it does on health care costs as these
people received NHS medical treatment when necessary anyway.
Disputes remain, and the British and American governments continue to make separate judgements. What the media have labelled
Gulf War syndrome, for example, allegedly suffered by some ser-
vicemen following action during the 1991 campaign against Iraq,
became officially recognized as an illness in America but campaigns
for recognition were still being resisted by the British government
in 1999, using the defence of the need for further research into the
condition.

Other associations have concentrated on the level of state
'investment' in disease eradication. In America much more than in
Britain, the ruse of publishing league tables of public spending on
basic research into particular diseases is a widely used lobbying
tactic by those associations feeling that the existing resource allocation is unfair. There is now quite a history of effective lobbying
resulting in last minute additions to capital budgets, earmarked for
research into specific conditions. President Clinton did this in the
case of diabetes in 1997, for example, in response to a mass letter-
writing campaign pointing out that the ratio of governmental
research support to direct disease costs was extremely low in comparison with a range of other conditions. Campaigners compared

diabetes figures with several others including arthritis, cancer, multiple sclerosis and dementia. It is notable that in a country where there is a strong belief in markets, the research budget of the National Institutes of Health has continued to grow steadily: in 1993, federal government medical research funding for the first time topped a staggering US$10 billion.

ASSOCIATIONS AS CONTRIBUTORS TO THE DEMOCRATIC POLITY?

In his pioneering study of 'intermediate organizations' (IOs), Alan Ware developed an overall analytical framework around 'identifying nine principal ways' in which IOs have been seen by democratic theorists as involved in the advancement of democratization (Ware 1989). Ware's list (see Table 10.1) was constructed to reflect several strands of pluralist theory, and it seeks to go well beyond the simple notion that the very existence of socio-political groups alone indicates that pluralism exists.

Ware's list of attributes is shared by one of the only two other British authors to relate patient groups to the concept of democracy (Ham (1977) was the third). Kendall and Knapp's criteria were briefer and less sophisticated (1996: 6). They cited observers of the charity sector as seeing this philanthropic activity as 'providing a voice for otherwise disadvantaged groups, providing a basis for countervailing power to both the state and the market, and offering developmental opportunities for political participation and control'

Table 10.1   Criteria to test associations' contribution to 'democracy'

1   They act as a countervailing force to the state and/or the market
2   They enhance public participation
3   They provide 'non-market goods'
4   They provide goods which the state or market does not offer or supply
5   They are 'safe' providers of service, with no interest in exploiting the recipients
6   They are more effective providers of goods and services than states or businesses
7   They help to cement the relationship between the state and society
8   They offer valuable diversity of opinion
9   They mobilize interests and demands in society

Source: Ware (1989: 12–21)

as their summary of Ware's nine criteria. We can conclude from the present study that the 500 patients' associations surveyed certainly do offer a 'voice' to the disadvantaged, given that many of the medical conditions they represent – some long term and chronic, others more episodical but equally distressing for the families affected – most certainly and clearly do disadvantage those with these conditions and their families and their carers.

Our evidence on the extent to which patients' associations in practice wield political power and influence has been less clear cut. We have certainly ascertained that patients' associations possess real political resources, but that many of them choose not to positively acquire or deploy them, opting instead to remain primarily as support rather than as campaigning groups. On the other hand, we also uncovered several examples of patients' associations influencing public policy – in the fields of mental illness and HIV/AIDS – and in successfully getting the state to recognize some medical conditions as being diseases. American successes in increasing state funding of basic research was also impressive.

It could be argued, though more tenuously, that the political rhetoric in both countries in the 1990s of consumer sovereignty and patients' rights also reflects an understanding by policy makers that patients' associations now have obtained political legitimacy and are entitled to be involved in the policy process. Finally, the impressive array of support services demonstrates much innovation and appears to support criteria 5 and 6 about non-exploitative and effective provision of goods and services.

Ware, however, it must be recalled was studying a far wider range of organizations than patients' associations, ranging through churches, private schools and non-state universities, and mutual benefit organizations such as trade unions, credit unions, social clubs and building and friendly societies as well as charities: all organizations which were either not part of the state or not permitted to distribute any profits earned fell within his remit and hence his interest in their relationship to states, society and democracy. Even so he concluded, somewhat reluctantly, that 'in many respects claims made by the democrats . . . about the contribution of IOs to the advancement of democracy cannot be substantiated' (Ware 1989: 256). In short, he felt that the nine criteria in Table 10.1 had not been met, or met only in part at best. It is now appropriate to use those same tests to evaluate the contribution towards democracy of our much narrower population group of disease-related patients' associations.

The evidence contained principally in Chapters 5–9 above allows us to be somewhat more upbeat than was Ware about our associations' contribution to the democratic polities of Britain and America. That they enhance public participation (criterion 2) seems particularly clear cut: in Chapter 4 we concluded that there are around 4 million American and 1 million British members of patients' associations, both impressive figures (they amount in each case to up to 2 per cent of the population. Recall also that earlier in this chapter we demonstrated that, whatever their claims, these associations are indeed highly political organizations.

Ware's next two criteria (3 and 4 in Table 10.1) relate to associations' outputs. It is hard to conceive of the market as an alternative provider of the range of basic support services, including advice and, crucially, reassurance, offered by associations to their members. The growth of telephone helplines is a particularly interesting instance of what is and is not capable of being provided by the market. Examples of association-operated helplines responding to very large numbers of queries were cited in Chapter 4; interesting because, as was then pointed out, Britain's Labour government decided to implement its decision to install a nationwide NHS direct helpline not through utilizing the considerable expertise to be found in patients' associations but rather by using the 'contract state' and inviting both non-profit and for-profit organizations to bid for contracts. NHS Helpline is costing around £54 million in the financial year 1999/2000 as it is rolled out area by area, with NHS ambulance services as the commonest headquarters, and the cost per call was high at the outset as levels of calls fell some way short of expectations. In Chapter 4 it was noted that, collectively, patients' associations spend around ten times that sum annually in Britain.

Ware's criterion 5, that groups do not want to exploit purchasers of their products, has to be assessed with some caution. This reflects the potential for, the consequences of, and indeed the extent of what we styled the 'professional colonization' of patients' associations. A particular problem relates to the codes of conduct and attitudes that associations may adopt (and many do not appear to have any written policies on this) towards potential benefactors and the consequent image of legitimacy that that may bestow on commercial organizations. In Chapter 5 the dependence of some associations on funds from the health technology industry was highlighted. Advertising in association newsletters is clearly an issue. To an ordinary member of an association the very fact that 'his' association accepts large advertisements from the provider of particular drugs or pieces of medical equipment which he might choose to buy has to be seen as, at the very least, indicating some implied level of approval by the association for the products concerned. Whether they like it or not, associations are giving to the public and their readers a public *appearance* of endorsing certain products and in so doing they enhance the sales and hence the profits of the manufacturers involved. There is surely some degree, however small, inherent in this process of at least potential exploitation of consumers, however innocent of that charge the associations involved may claim to be. After all, we have several times referred to the political importance of values and of belief systems in the politics of health: in this instance beliefs can be more important than 'facts' in influencing the purchasing behaviour of members – the very people the associations are actually seeking to protect and to represent.

That autonomous organizations help to cement the state/society relationship (criterion 7) is at the centre of most pluralist thinking (Ware 1989: 256–7; Kendall and Knapp 1996: 6), and in the mid-1990s several academic thinkers began to express concerns about the alleged disappearance of what is usually labelled as 'social capital'. One to go public on 'the decline of community in contemporary America' was Harvard's senior professor, Robert Putnam, arguing *inter alia* in a prestigious public lecture, that 'political discourse . . . had been impaired by the decline of social interaction' because new technology like television promoted individualism at the expense of community activity (Putnam 1995: 680–1; for a riposte on the particular argument about the influence of television see Norris (1996)). The relevance of this debate to Ware's test of democratic health lies in the methodology employed and deployed by Putnam, who relied heavily on public self-reporting of group memberships in responses to the American General Social Survey data for the period 1989–94. Having defined social capital as being a 'network of norms and social trust by which people pursued shared objectives through their memberships of social, economic and other voluntary bodies', Putnam was alarmed to unearth data which indicated sharply declining membership levels and numbers of such groups and of other local forms of collective political participation. Putnam's explanations included the role of television in promoting individualism at the expense of social interaction, with a consequent destruction of social capital.

Putnam's evidence proved to be, in part, technically wrong, and

a year later he published corrected reworked time-series membership data which increased membership levels by about 15 per cent
though still claiming that 'the advent of television had a marked
negative effect on the civic engagement of the post-war generation
of Americans' (Helliwell and Putnam 1996). His data analysis was
through 16 categories of group, ranging from 'hobby/garden' to
'church' and 'labor unions'. However, in both the original and the
reworked data he had, from the outset, no category for health
groups, nor, more surprisingly, were there categories covering
either social welfare or disability. From the material in this book
alone we are now in a strong position to conclude that, had Putnam
made any attempt to include a category that included patients'
associations and other collective support groups in the health and
welfare fields, that category would inevitably have reflected this
survey's findings of burgeoning numbers of such groups and of
large-scale global memberships.

   In the light of this record of public participation in great numbers
it is difficult to conclude other than that patients' associations do
indeed meet Ware's two criteria (7 and 9) on state/society relations
and on helping to mobilize opinion and demands even if, as Ham
has noted, there remain 'inequalities between producer [meaning
doctors for example] and consumer groups' (Ham 1977: 117). Society in Britain, for example, now expects there to be an annual
Marie Curie day and other similar flag days as a focus for mass
fund-raising activities, and thousands of sponsored runners in the
annual London Marathon and Great North Race. Such activity by
charity fund-raising enthusiasts has become part of the routine of
the accepted socio-political landscape in Britain.

   It is, however, necessary to conclude with a degree of caution in
relation to Ware's criterion number 8 and the value of expressions of
diversity of opinion. Early on we identified the existence of competing groups seeking to represent the same medical condition (Chapter 3 discussed this phenomenon at some length). Explanations of
this perhaps surprising degree of competition could include important disputes about fundamentals, including competing theories of
the efficacy of particular treatment regimes such as the balance
between community or compulsory institutional care in the case of
certain psychiatric diagnoses or the relative merits of biomedical or
herbal regimes in the treatment of some conditions. Although exemplars of these and other clinical disagreements were offered, with a
special emphasis on the disputes about psychiatric care systems, it
was also clear that many of the apparently competing groups really

had no strong separate philosophy of their own to underpin their activities and demands, and a good deal of the competition was more about campaigning for orthodox medicine to recognize and accept certain diseases than it was about treatment regimes. In short, orthodox medicine has such a strong hold in both countries that serious debate between it and complementary therapies or other alternative health care regimes was not convincingly unearthed through this study of patients' associations: hence the extent of diversity of opinions represented by patients' associations is limited by their choosin to act within the boundaries of orthodox (or allopathic) medicine.

DESIGNING 'EFFECTIVENESS INDICATORS'

How efficient and politically effective are disease-related patients' associations? These two questions were the original driving force behind this study and yet, at the end of the exercise the conclusions that we have been able to draw from the material remain limited and tentative in nature. It is perfectly reasonable for the reader to ask why such apparent uncertainty should exist after a two-year research project involving questionnaire surveys and interviews as well as the orthodox research methods of literature search and synthesis of material.

Measuring effectiveness in any context is always tricky. The concept appears initially to be quite straightforward: the effective organization (or person, event or public policy) is the one which meets its objectives at reasonable cost. Patients' associations as political organizations should, to be deemed effective, exert political influence and conduct their affairs economically and efficiently. Yet, at the end of the day, measuring their performance remains tantalizingly elusive because we lack robust comparators of performance against which to judge them. In short, the great gap in the (relatively few) authoritative studies of the voluntary sector is precisely that researchers have yet to attempt to construct a series of 'performance indicators' for philanthropic organizations of the type that have been developed in areas of public policy as diverse as education, health care and garbage collection.

The opening and final sentences of books have always been a problem for authors. Drafting of this chapter began on the assumption that a final section of it might well be headed 'future research agenda'. As this is the first ever across-the-board comparative study of patients' associations as political organizations, that seemed appropriate. This plan began to be amended when a rereading of Chapters 1–9 revealed that they developed a myriad of potential areas for further research and collectively constitute an ambitious ongoing research agenda, with every chapter throwing up topics worthy of further investigation as is inevitable in any pioneering broad-brush study of a new political phenomenon. There indeed remains much to be done before we can fully understand the politics of patient groups and their impact on health care systems and public policies. In a world as fast-changing as this one was found to be, even the most basic descriptive materials about associations are already badly dated.

In Chapters 1–9 and earlier in this one a number of possible 'performance indicators' have begun to emerge. Even so, the data to illustrate them would require a great deal of research to ensure their robustness, not least because the general approach in earlier chapters was one of accepting material presented by associations as accurate, given that it was supplied in good faith and respondents had no knowledge as to whether this would result in a 'friendly' or a 'hostile' study of these health charities.

Probably the greatest concerns to the general public about these associations emerged in Chapter 5 on the associations' political economy. The implicit criticism that some associations might be deemed to be 'high cost' bodies points to the desirability of published indicators about their financial performance. Obvious examples include the proportion of income or expenditure devoted to what were labelled as 'overheads': to administrative and management costs, and to the costs of fund-raising activities. The 25 per cent benchmark used in Chapter 5 was clearly constructed somewhat arbitrarily, nevertheless the numbers of outliers that were thrown up by applying it to the published accounts of patients' associations was rather disturbing. In addition to that, potential individual donors would not be reassured by the fact that several of the apparently costliest outliers named at that point publicly claimed to be economically run organizations. Indeed, some cited as spending 30, 40 or even 50 per cent of their income on 'overheads' were claiming that over 90 per cent of donations were spent directly on the provision of services or relief of people with the condition represented. A set of 'league tables' on the finances of health charities is badly needed, and it might consist of several indicators including the proportion of income raised from individual donations (proposed by Gutch (1999)) as well as the ratio of 'overheads' to income.

In addition to financial indicators, which could well reassure the general public about the excellent work which many associations do and highlight good management practice, there is also a case for work to be done on constructing indicators of political performance. This is much more difficult for several reasons, not least because influence is not something that can clearly be assigned to any specific moment in time, be it a year or a month. Take the field of mental health where researchers and policy makers generally accept that patients' associations have indeed been influential. Few would offer as an example of this any particular public policy pronouncement or legislative or budgetary initiative. Rather, the presence in Britain of advocacy organizations like MIND, SANE, and the National Schizophrenia Fellowship has kept services for the mentally ill high on the political health agenda now for a generation, and at various times all three and other charities in this field have worked closely enough with government on taskforces and enquiries that they illustrate incorporation. The difficulty lies in designing performance indicators which truly represent their stake in policy making, though one might be the extent to which government does use them to man its network of advisory bodies (Ham (1977: 109–12) effectively illustrates debate at that time about the tactics of MIND and debates about its campaigning activities). Other political indicators might include involvement in political alliances and coalitions, activities relating to parliament and congress (several instances of associations actively persuading friendly MPs to establish all-party committees would emerge), and expenditures of staff time and of money on overt campaigning.

A final set of indicators would relate to internal institutional performance. In both countries many annual reports of associations currently fail to include basic data about the role of the board and of its unpaid members or directors. Even the minimum of attendance records at meetings of board and of its committees are absent; so is the amount of expenses paid out. There is no indication of how active members are, either in meetings or between meetings (in the case of the larger associations, for example, on how many occasions its services were visited or the numbers of branches and their functions attended). Because annual reports are designed to announce 'good' news first and foremost, publication of such information might require an agreed code of conduct or necessitate a series of case studies to construct. The importance of possessing an active board is such that several associations in both Britain and America admitted openly that recruiting 'good' board members was problematic, and the St Louis and Manchester case studies threw up some instances of inactive boards with some associations in effect moribund. There clearly is a need to develop what are here labelled EIs (effectiveness indicators) not just for patients' associations but across the charity sector if only to reassure the public about its contribution to modern democracy.

The world of patients' associations was found to be one which continues to be fast-moving, indeed hard even to chart accurately at any point in time. This continues to be the case, and to illustrate it this book ends with an interesting instance which arose as this chapter was being drafted and which reinforces the need for further case studies to be undertaken to explore the general points made in this book.

The instance relates to a general point made more than once earlier, including in the two conurbation case studies, about the indications that active patients' associations appear to relate to social class and wealth. Certain medical conditions are more respectable than others in society, and these emerged as being more strongly represented (chronic fatigue syndrome and ME come immediately to mind) than are working-class ailments like sickle cell disease. In Britain in March 1999 yet another new association was launched (nothing very odd here given the rate of growth reported in Chapter 3) but somewhat unusually it seeks to campaign against an illness particularly prevalent in the poorest communities: tuberculosis. TB Alert claimed to be 'the first UK TB charity since the 1960s'. It consciously adopted the typical characteristics of associations as described in Chapter 4: launched at Westminster with lists of prominent supporters including the junior minister who launched it; offices close to central London, and so on. It chose to overlook the interest of some other associations in tuberculosis and its historical claim chose to ignore, for example, the (1980s) British Lung Foundation (BLF) which, amongst other activities included in 1997 the sponsorship of a professorship at Edinburgh University and awards of research grants topping £1 million for the first time in its history. BLF's six regional offices run a network of branches styled Breathe Easy Groups, and its simple and readable factsheet on tuberculosis is published in seven languages. It will be interesting to monitor TB Alert's success in mobilizing poor communities, in managing to establish a network of active branches in impoverished areas of Britain and in acquiring and deploying political resources in its battle against what at launch was said to be a 'Killer disease out of control'.

Very finally, an unfortunate and unexpected episode of personal illness during final drafting of this book led me to seek advice from the UK Stroke Association. Earlier cited as being politically effective, it fully lived up to the implication that it was also an efficient organization, as indeed are the vast majority of associations studied (as revealed alone by the response rate to my postal survey of over 80 per cent in Britain, and that proportion was already over 70 per cent when reminders were sent out). To whoever was manning the UK Stroke Association's helpline that day in March 1999 when I received very welcome support and reassurance about my changed health status, with useful literature posted out immediately, I can only end by saying this: 'Thank you very much indeed, and keep up the good work that you are doing.' The same message applies to almost all of the other 450 or so associations we have examined in this monograph.

REFERENCES

Alderman, G. (1984). *Pressure Groups and Government in Great Britain.* Harlow: Longman.

Alford, R. (1975). *Health Care Politics.* Chicago: University of Chicago Press.

Allison, L. (1975). *Environmental Planning.* London: Allen & Unwin.

Allsop, J. (1995). *Health Policy and the NHS: Towards 2000.* London: Longman.

Association of Medical Research Charities (AMRC) (1997). *Handbook 1997–1998.* London: AMRC.

Baggott, R. (1995). *Pressure Groups Today.* Manchester: Manchester University Press.

Baggott, R. (1998). *Health and Health Care in Britain*, 2nd edn. Basingstoke: Macmillan.

Bakal, C. (1979). *Charity, USA.* New York: Times Books.

Bennett, J.T. and Dilorenzo, T.J. (1994). *Unhealthy Charities.* New York: Basic Books.

Berridge, V. (1996). *AIDS in the UK: the Making of Policy.* Oxford: Oxford University Press.

Dalton, R.J. and Kuechler, M. (eds) (1990). *Challenging the Political Order: New Social and Political Movements in Western Democracies.* Cambridge: Polity Press.

Easton, D. (1953). *The Political System.* New York: Knopf.

Elston, M.A. (1991). The politics of professional power: medicine in a changing health service. In J. Gabe, M. Calnan and M. Bury (eds) *The Sociology of the Health Service.* London: Routledge.

Finer, S.E. (1966). *Anonymous Empire*, 2nd edn. London: Pall Mall.

Fox, P. (1989). From senility to Alzheimer's disease: the rise of the Alzheimer's disease movement. *Millbank Quarterly*, 67, 58–102.

Gutch, R. (1999). Making waves, *The Guardian*, 21 April.

Ham, C. (1977). Power, patients and pluralism. In K. Barnard and K. Lee (eds) *Conflicts in the National Health Service.* London: Croom Helm.

Harris, M. (1998). Instruments of government? Voluntary sector boards in a changing public policy environment. *Policy and Politics*, 26(2), 177–88.

Harrison, S. (1999). Clinical autonomy and health policy: past and futures. In M. Exworthy and S. Halford (eds) *Professionalism and the New Managerialism in the Public Sector*. Buckingham: Open University Press.

Harrison, S. and Mort, M. (1998). Which champions, which people? Public and user involvement in health care as a technology of legitimation. *Social Policy and Administration*, 32(1), 60–70.

Harrison, S., Barnes, M. and Mort, M. (1997). Praise and damnation: mental health user groups and the construction of organisational legitimacy. *Public Policy and Administration*, 12(2), 17–30.

Helliwell, J.F. and Putnam, R.D. (1996). Correction. *PS: Political Science and Politics*, 29(1), 138.

Hunter, D.J. (1994). From tribalism to corporatism: the managerial challenge to medical dominance. In J. Gabe, D. Kelleher and G. Williams (eds) *Challenging Medicine*. London: Routledge.

Kelleher, D. (1991). Patients learning from each other: self-help groups for people with diabetes. *Journal of the Royal Society of Medicine*, 84, 595–7.

Kelleher, D. (1994). Self-help groups and their relationship to medicine. In J. Gabe, D. Kelleher and G. Williams (eds) *Challenging Medicine*. London: Routledge.

Kendall, J. and Knapp, M. (1996). *The Voluntary Sector in the UK*. Manchester: Manchester University Press.

Lewthwaite, J. and Haffenden, S. (1997). *Patients Influencing Purchasers*. Birmingham: NHS Confederation.

Manning, N. and Shaw, I. (eds) (1999). Special Issue: Mental Health and Social Order. *Policy and Politics*, 27(1).

Mechanic, D. (1991). Sources of countervailing power in medicine. *Journal of Health Politics, Policy and Law*, 16(3), 485–98.

Moran, M. (1989). *Politics and Society in Britain*, 2nd edn. Basingstoke: Macmillan.

Moran, M. (1998). Explaining the rise of the market in health care. In W. Ranade (ed.) *Markets and Health Care: a Comparative Analysis*. London: Longman.

Moran, M. and Wood, B. (1993). *States, Regulation and the Medical Profession*. Buckingham: Open University Press.

National Audit Office (1987). *Monitoring and Control of Charities in England and Wales*. London: HMSO.

NHS Management Executive (1992). *Local Voices: Views of Local People in Purchasing for Health*. London: HMSO.

Norris, P. (1996). Does television erode social capital? A reply to Putnam. *PS: Political Science and Politics*, 29(3), 474–80.

Olson, M. (1965). *The Logic of Collective Action*. Cambridge, MA: Harvard University Press.

Patel, K. and Rushefsky, M.E. (1995). *Health Care Politics and Policy in America*. Armonk, NY: M.E. Sharpe.

Peterson, M. (1993). Institutional change and the health politics of the 1990s. *American Behavioral Scientist*, 36(6), 782–801.

Philpot, T. and Hanvey, C. (1996). *Sweet Charity: The Role and Workings of Voluntary Associations.* London: Routledge.

Polsby, N.W. (1963). *Community Power and Political Theory.* New Haven, CT: Yale University Press.

Powell, M. (1998). In what sense a *National* Health Service? *Public Policy and Administration*, 13(3), 56–69.

Putnam, R.D. (1995). Tuning in, tuning out: the strange disappearance of social capital in America. *PS: Political Science and Politics*, 28(4), 664–83.

Rettig, R.A. (1994). Medical innovation duels cost containment. *Health Affairs*, 13(3), 7–27.

Rhodes, R.P. (1996). Review of 'health care politics and policy in America'. *American Political Science Review*, 90(2), 436–7.

Royal College of Physicians (1999). *Stroke Rehabilitation: Patient and Carer Views.* London: RCP.

Secretary of State for Health (1997). *The New NHS: Modern, Dependable*, Cm. 3807. London: HMSO.

Skocpol, T. (1996). *Boomerang: Clinton's Health Security Efforts and the Turn Against Government in US Politics.* New York: W.W. Norton.

Stewart, J.D. (1958). *British Pressure Groups.* Oxford: Clarendon Press.

Walt, G. (1994). *Health Policy.* London: Zed Books.

Wann, M. (1995). *Building Social Capital: Self-help in a Twenty-first Century Welfare State.* London: Institute for Public Policy Research.

Ware, A. (1989). *Between Profit and State: Intermediate Organisations in Britain and the United States.* Cambridge: Polity Press.

Weeks, J. and Aggleton, P.J. (1994). *Voluntary Sector Responses to HIV/AIDS: Policies, Principles and Practice.* Swindon: ESRC End of Award Report no. R–000–23–3669–01.

Weissert, C.S. and Weissert, W.G. (1996). *Governing Health: the Politics of Health Policy.* Baltimore, MD: Johns Hopkins University Press.

White, P. (1999). Invalid criticism? *The Guardian*, 21 April.

Whiteley, P.F. and Winyard, S.J. (1987). *Pressure for the Poor.* London: Methuen.

Williams, G. (1989). Hope for the humblest? The role of self-help in chronic illness: the case of ankylosing spondylitis. *Sociology of Health and Illness*, 11, 135–59.

Wilson, J. (1995). *How to Work with Self-help Groups.* Aldershot: Ashgate.

Wood, B. (1995). Federalism, implementation and equity: the importance of place in American health care reform. *Health and Place*, 1(1), 61–4.

Note: for information about the associations surveyed contact the author, Bruce Wood, Dean of the Faculty of Economic and Social Studies, University of Manchester, Oxford Road, Manchester, M13 9PL, UK.

INDEX OF ASSOCIATIONS

SUBJECT INDEX

DEMANDING PATIENTS?
ANALYSING THE USE OF PRIMARY CARE

Anne Rogers, Karen Hassell and Gerry Nicolaas

The management of demand for healthcare is a central concern to policy makers, commissioners and providers. Only a small proportion of health problems experienced by people living in the community result in contact with healthcare professionals in primary or secondary care. As a consequence small changes in the health actions of the public or in the accessibility of a service are likely to produce large changes in workload and create dilemmas for health policy makers charged with meeting need in a resource constrained healthcare system. This book brings together concepts, policy issues and recent research findings on help-seeking and healthcare utilization. It focuses on lay decision making and examines the influences and factors shaping the relationship between health need and demand for care by examining the connections between people's experience of health problems, their care for themselves and their use of formal health care and community pharmacy.

Contents

272pp   0 335 20090 7 (Paperback)   0 335 20091 5 (Hardback)

REFORMING MARKETS IN HEALTH CARE
AN ECONOMIC PERSPECTIVE
Peter C. Smith (ed.)

There has been an international move towards the creation of explicit markets in health care, in which the purchase of care is separated from provision. While the creation of such markets has undeniably led to improvements in certain aspects of health care, it has also raised important issues that have yet to be resolved – for example, is an escalation of management costs an inevitable consequence of the introduction of a market in health care? What sort of information is needed to make the market function efficiently? Can a market-based system be compatible with society's objectives relating to equity and solidarity? The UK government is introducing reforms to the internal health care market in the UK National Health Service which seek to address concerns such as these, and this book comprises a series of commentaries on their plans from a group of leading health economists. Authors examine the contribution of economics to the debate on the reforms, while seeking to make the analysis accessible to a general audience.

Reforming Markets in Health Care is recommended reading for students and researchers of health policy and health economics, as well as health professionals and policy makers at all levels in the health services.

Contents

320pp   0 335 20461 9 (Paperback)   0 335 20462 7 (Hardback)

THE GLOBAL CHALLENGE OF HEALTH CARE RATIONING

Angela Coulter and Chris Ham (eds)

Rationing or priority setting occurs in all health care systems. Doctors, managers, and politicians are involved in making decisions on how to use scarce resources and which groups and patients should receive priority. These decisions may be informed by the results of medical research and cost effectiveness studies but they also involve the use of judgement and experience. Consequently, priority setting involves ethics as well as economics and decisions on who should live and who should die remain controversial and contested.

This book seeks to illuminate the debate on priority setting by drawing on experience from around the world. The authors are all involved in priority setting, either as decision makers or researchers, and their contributions demonstrate in practical terms how different countries and disciplines are approaching the allocation of resources between competing claims. Accessible to general readers as well as specialists, *The Global Challenge of Health Care Rationing* summarizes the latest thinking in this area and provides a unique resource for those searching for a guide through the maze.

Contents

c. 228pp   0 335 20463 5 (Paperback)   0 335 20464 3 (Hardback)